The Design of Things to Come

How Ordinary People Create Extraordinary Products

Ideas. Action. Impact.
**Wharton School
Publishing**

In the face of accelerating turbulence and change, business leaders and policy makers need new ways of thinking to sustain performance and growth.

Wharton School Publishing offers a trusted source for stimulating ideas from thought leaders who provide new mental models to address changes in strategy, management, and finance. We seek out authors from diverse disciplines with a profound understanding of change and its implications. We offer books and tools that help executives respond to the challenge of change.

Every book and management tool we publish meets quality standards set by The Wharton School of the University of Pennsylvania. Each title is reviewed by the Wharton School Publishing Editorial Board before being given Wharton's seal of approval. This ensures that Wharton publications are timely, relevant, important, conceptually sound or empirically based, and implementable.

To fit our readers' learning preferences, Wharton publications are available in multiple formats, including books, audio, and electronic.

To find out more about our books and management tools, visit us at whartonsp.com and Wharton's executive education site, exceed.wharton.upenn.edu.

The Design of Things to Come

How Ordinary People Create Extraordinary Products

Craig M. Vogel
Jonathan Cagan
Peter Boatwright

Ideas. Action. Impact.
Wharton School Publishing

Library of Congress Catalog Number: 2005920661

Publisher: Tim Moore
Executive Editor: Jim Boyd
Editorial Assistant: Kate E. Stephenson
Development Editor: Russ Hall
Marketing Manager: Martin Litkowski
International Marketing Manager: Tim Galligan
Cover Designer: Alan Clements
Managing Editor: Gina Kanouse
Project Editor: Rose Sweazy
Copy Editor: Keith Cline
Indexer: Larry Sweazy
Senior Compositor: Gloria Schurick
Manufacturing Buyer: Dan Uhrig
Art Illustrator: Shane Machir
Additional art by Lisa Troutman

 Ideas. Action. Impact.
Wharton School Publishing

© 2005 by Pearson Education, Inc.
Publishing as Wharton School Publishing
Upper Saddle River, New Jersey 07458

Wharton School Publishing offers excellent discounts on this book when ordered in quantity for bulk purchases or special sales. For more information, please contact U.S. Corporate and Government Sales, 1-800-382-3419, corpsales@pearsontechgroup.com. For sales outside the U.S., please contact International Sales at international@pearsoned.com.

Printed in the United States of America

First Printing April 2005

ISBN 0-131-86082-8

Pearson Education Ltd.
Pearson Education Australia PTY, Ltd.
Pearson Education Singapore, Pte. Ltd.
Pearson Education North Asia, Ltd.
Pearson Education Canada, Ltd.
Pearson Educatión de Mexico, S.A. de C.V.
Pearson Education—Japan
Pearson Education Malaysia, Pte. Ltd.

Ideas. Action. Impact.
Wharton School Publishing

Bernard Baumohl
THE SECRETS OF ECONOMIC INDICATORS
Hidden Clues to Future Economic Trends and Investment Opportunities

Sayan Chatterjee
FAILSAFE STRATEGIES
Profit and Grow from Risks That Others Avoid

Sunil Gupta, Donald R. Lehmann
MANAGING CUSTOMERS AS INVESTMENTS
The Strategic Value of Customers in the Long Run

Stuart L. Hart
CAPITALISM AT THE CROSSROADS
The Unlimited Business Opportunities in Solving the World's Most Difficult Problems

Lawrence G. Hrebiniak
MAKING STRATEGY WORK
Leading Effective Execution and Change

Robert Mittelstaedt
WILL YOUR NEXT MISTAKE BE FATAL?
Avoiding the Chain of Mistakes That Can Destroy Your Organization

Mukul Pandya, Robbie Shell, Susan Warner, Sandeep Junnarkar, Jeffrey Brown
NIGHTLY BUSINESS REPORT PRESENTS LASTING LEADERSHIP
What You Can Learn from the Top 25 Business People of Our Times

C. K. Prahalad
THE FORTUNE AT THE BOTTOM OF THE PYRAMID
Eradicating Poverty Through Profits

Scott A. Shane
FINDING FERTILE GROUND
Identifying Extraordinary Opportunities for New Ventures

Oded Shenkar
THE CHINESE CENTURY
The Rising Chinese Economy and Its Impact on the Global Economy, the Balance of Power, and Your Job

David Sirota, Louis A. Mischkind, and Michael Irwin Meltzer
THE ENTHUSIASTIC EMPLOYEE
How Companies Profit by Giving Workers What They Want

Thomas T. Stallkamp
SCORE!
A Better Way to Do Busine$$: Moving from Conflict to Collaboration

Yoram (Jerry)Wind, Colin Crook, with Robert Gunther
THE POWER OF IMPOSSIBLE THINKING
Transform the Business of Your Life and the Life of Your Business

To Elizabeth, Melissa, Joshua, Benjamin, Annabel, and Brayden—next-generation innovators

TABLE OF CONTENTS

FOREWORD

If there is one lesson from the dot-com craze and meltdown that will endure (until the next time, anyway), it was this: A great idea is not the same thing as a great innovation.

We saw some truly fabulous ideas come over the transom here at *Fast Company*: There was, for a few shining months, balls.com, proud 24/7 purveyor of any sports ball you could imagine, and gesundheit.com, offering comprehensive relief for the allergy sufferer. But these late, mostly forgotten sites didn't deliver much in the way of value. People didn't need this stuff—not enough, anyway, to pay the bills. Ordering pet food online and having it delivered to your home was a terrific idea, but—no disrespect to the sock puppet—it just wasn't pragmatic.

Now consider Google, a dot-com survivor (needless to say) whose dedication to innovation verges on the maniacal. A Google engineer once explained to me the calculus behind temporarily adding a brief pitch—"New! Take your search further. Take a Google Tour"—to the site's otherwise austere home page. Those nine words, Google knew, comprised 120 bytes of data, which would slow download times for people with modems by 20 to 50 milliseconds. But Google could also measure precisely how many visitors took the tour, downloaded the Google Toolbar, and clicked through for the first time to Google News.

At Google, an idea that provides no demonstrable value to customers just doesn't happen. The company is constantly testing new features on its site. The ones that people use, that don't degrade the search experience, and that fit the business strategy—those are the ones that stick. The others—well, they're just ideas, and they disappear. "We don't show people things that they aren't interested in," said another engineer, "because in the long run, that will kill your business."

The gearheads at Google are pragmatic innovators—exactly the sort that Craig Vogel, Jonathan Cagan, and Peter Boatwright describe in this book. They understand that innovation isn't defined solely (or sometimes, at all) by daring acts of technological invention. Innovation is, instead, about providing advances that are valued by customers.

The difference between the two was brought home to me several years ago in Craig's office, then (and, I assume, still) a crowded reliquary positioned at the intersection of creative destruction and consumerism. The shelves were packed with old rotary telephones, radios, coffeemakers, toasters, and Coke cans.

And with potato peelers. Here was the "Rotato Potato Peeler," a mechanical marvel that applied high tech to the low art of removing a tuber's skin. It worked—but it was cumbersome and ugly, and it removed an eighth of an inch of potato flesh. The seven-dollar OXO peeler, by contrast, was just an incremental advance on the century-old mechanical standard. But that increment—a more comfortable handle, a curved blade, a cleaner look—was valuable. It turned the mundane into something enjoyable, even beautiful.

That's the ballgame today. Not, What can you make? Not even, What can you make that people will buy? But, What can you make that will add enough value to people's lives to sell profitably? That's why one of the coauthors of this book is a marketing guy.

Pay special attention in the pages that follow to the consumer profiles that introduce each chapter. They're important, because they acquaint us with the central players in any discussion of innovation—the people who buy and use your products. Note that they are not just wealthy, well-educated professionals. Consumers of all stripes have become, in the last two decades, remarkably savvy about design and its value in our lives. If this book is about "how ordinary people create extraordinary products," it's also about how ordinary people have become design nuts. Call us the Target Generation.

It's all too easy for companies to forget about their customers—and easy as well to spot the results. (The Rotato! Just $19.99!) Do this, obviously, at your peril: A new product strategy is not complete unless you understand who these people are, how your innovation will improve their lives, and what that change is worth to them.

If you don't, some nimbler competitor surely will. Motorola and Nokia dominated the growing Chinese cell phone market for years—until a local outfit, Ningbo Bird, became a pragmatic innovator. Instead of producing phones that were simply cheap, Ningbo Bird began studying what Chinese consumers wanted—and making phones that were sexy and easy to use. Its market share jumped from 5 percent to over 50 percent in just a few years.

So, which is it? Is your company a Ningbo Bird, or a Motorola? An OXO, or a Rotato? A Google, or a gezundheit.com? This book will help you understand your customers and then create products and services that they want, products and services that are likely to be great innovations and not just ideas.

Keith H. Hammonds

Deputy Editor, *Fast Company* magazine

ABOUT THE AUTHORS

Craig M. Vogel is a professor in the School of Design and director of the Center for Design Research and Innovation in the college of Design Architecture, Art and Planning at the University of Cincinnati. He has developed an approach to design that integrates teaching and research. He has worked with a variety of companies as a consultant for new product development and strategic planning.

Jonathan Cagan, Ph.D., P.E., is a professor of mechanical engineering at Carnegie Mellon University. His research, teaching, and extensive consulting focus on product development, strategic planning, and design. He has developed team-based tools and computer-based technologies to improve the process of design conceptualization.

Photo by Larry Rippel

Peter Boatwright, Ph.D., is associate professor of marketing in the Tepper School of Business at Carnegie Mellon University. His expertise and teaching focus on new product marketing, consumer marketing, and marketing research methods. In his research, Professor Boatwright has developed new statistical methods, as well as additional theories of consumer behavior.

Photo by Larry Rippel

The authors have worked with a variety of companies, including, Procter & Gamble, International Truck and Engine, Respironics, Alcoa, Kennametal, New Balance, Kraft Foods, Motorola, Lubrizol, Ford, General Motors, Whirlpool, RedZone Robotics, DesignAdvance Systems, and Exxon Chemical.

Professors Cagan and Vogel are coauthors of the book *Creating Breakthrough Products*, which is a detailed approach to navigating the fuzzy front end of product development.

ABOUT THE COVER

Burnie is our animated robotic toaster, the one on the book cover. You may be wondering why we put Burnie there, since he is not a real product like the others in this book. These days, if a product team walked into the office of their VP of New Product and said, "We have just developed the world's first walking toaster!" the answer might be "Great! But can it walk on water?" Burnie represents the incredible requests made of teams and individuals working in the area of new product and service development. A walking toaster may or may not be what the public wants, nor may it fit a company's strategic plan. The question is, "How do you know?"

In this book, we give many examples of real products. The teams developed these products only after fully understanding their customers' needs, assessing the strength and boundaries of their company's brand, considering how and how far they could extend the brand, and thinking of their company's strategic needs for innovation and organic growth. A smart shoe, a device for cleaning floors without water, a robot that is not a toaster but that does repair sewer systems, and a pickup truck that fulfills fantasy expectations are part of the array of case studies and their corresponding methods of development we provide to enable you to make the right choice in the design of things to come.

PREFACE

What to Expect from This Book

Two guys walk into a Starbucks and wave to a woman at a table. After getting their lattes, they head over and join her.

Paul: Hey, Caroline, looks like you got here early.

Caroline: Traffic wasn't bad today. Did you two come together?

Rick: No. We just happened to arrive at the same time. How are you doing? How's work?

Caroline: It's pretty interesting these days. Today we had a planning meeting to set objectives for the next few quarters. We had a poor performance last year, and budgets are getting cut. I was asked to reduce cost by 20 percent and increase profits by 150 percent. [She smiles.]

Paul: Are these just goals to see how high you can jump? Or are they somewhat realistic?

Caroline: It's part of an ongoing internal discussion. We've gotten really efficient at delivering high quality with decent costs. But, you know, everybody else is pretty good at it now. So the discussion is about what to do next. For years, we've had the dual strategy of beefing up quality and reducing costs, and that strategy has worked well for us. But now, we're pretty close to the efficient frontier, and everyone else is catching up pretty quickly.

Rick: I know what you mean. We're lost as to how to respond to the latest competitor who is trying to drag everyone into a death rattle on price. It isn't like there is much more we can do with our manufacturing costs or quality. I am a black belt Six Sigma, and we've integrated the latest on lean manufacturing into our StageGate process. Now that we're accustomed to putting out high quality at low cost, we've settled back into our old bunkers. The sales force is on our back to put out some new product that can compete on cost. But we're putting out great stuff, so we wonder why sales can't move product by just showing buyers our quality difference.

           Paul, now that I think about it, you guys don't seem to be in this cost battle at the moment. You guys are thinking innovation instead of costs, aren't you?

Paul: Yeah, I told you guys about the new CEO a while back. He has a different focus. Still too early to tell what will happen, but I have to say that there's excitement in the air that wasn't there before. He believes that we can no longer compete on price but instead need to be leaders in innovation. A couple of weeks ago, he sent out a memo with suggested reading. I read an article in *Business Week* about the power of design. Usually, articles about design just talk about industrial design and how they make products better. But this article was different. It said that product design means that everyone has to be innovative, not just the industrial designers you hire. Another article talked about the challenge of the growth of China, stressing how companies in Asia are getting smarter, not just cheaper, and that means innovation is the only way to compete. He also sent some literature about programs that a number of B schools are teaching on "entrepreneurship and innovation." He is actually willing to support us getting into those programs. Even he admits the innovation seminars we are constantly attending can only get us to the beginning of what we need to do.

I've not yet read the book *The Design of Things to Come* that he suggested, but I've heard it has some pragmatic ideas on creating profit and growth by focusing on customer needs and desires, and that it has techniques that any of us can understand and incorporate into our process....

Deconstructing Innovation

Everyone is talking and writing about innovation. It is the fuel of business strategy. Design and innovation are words that are often used together or interchangeably. Design for us is both a broad concept of change through human problem solving and a word used to describe specific fields such as engineering design, interface design, or industrial design. The power of the new design for innovation is fueling an engine of change that is driving the production of things to come. It is the result of interdisciplinary teams, and it dynamically leads to comprehensive solutions that consumers respond to emotionally, cognitively, and then economically. Few books, however, provide an understanding of how to deconstruct the process in a way that anyone can use to turn a cost-centric approach into an innovation-driven strategy. The challenge in design for innovation is to help everyday people stretch and grow to accomplish extraordinary things.

As authors from three different disciplines, we are strongly committed to understanding the innovative process. We represent three core areas that companies rely on for innovation of physical products: business, engineering, and industrial design. As a result of our diversity and commitment to the topic, we believe it is possible to provide a distinct useful, usable, and desirable angle on the current trend of how companies are growing organically through innovation. We have developed an ability to see current and emerging issues through three sets of eyes translated into one common transdisciplinary voice. The result is something that can educate the novice and help experienced practitioners in business alike. The potential in companies is not just the ability to create a pool of talent and capability, but how to give diverse teams of people the power, methods, and courage to be creative and to explore new opportunities. As our own example of the power of teams, writing this book required significant give and take for each of us as individuals. The result is a product that is better than any one of us could have written in isolation.

In our roles as university professors, our work has evolved into a balance of research, consulting, and teaching that has allowed us to become an example of what we talk about in the book. We are not just reporting what we have observed; we have lived it. We know what it is like to manage interdisciplinary teams of bright, headstrong people and help them produce innovative and patentable solutions through our methods. We have impressed company executives with the ability to take a vague discussion of possible new markets and, using an integrated product development process in a university context, produce insightful, thoroughly developed and patented products. We have consulted with a wide variety of consumer and business-to-business companies and helped them produce successful products. The first book of two of the authors, *Creating Breakthrough Products*[1], has been incorporated into the product development process of many small and large companies alike.

1   Cagan, J. and C. M. Vogel. *Creating Breakthrough Products: Innovation from Product Planning to Program Approval*. Financial Times Prentice Hall, Upper Saddle River, NJ, 2002.

As research professors, we have had the opportunity to step back and reflect on what we have observed. We have identified consistent patterns that led to successful innovation. Our goal as writers was to produce a book that organizes and expresses these findings in a way that the Carolines, Ricks, and Pauls of the preceding vignette can incorporate into their way of thinking and practice. In short, it is a book written by people who have lived with, successfully managed, and thoroughly researched the topic. Said another way, we are armchair quarterbacks who have also played the game.

This book deconstructs innovation into understandable chunks that form a compelling argument of what innovation is, why it is important, and how you can begin to transform yourself and your company to meet the needs of the current marketplace. You cannot just hire innovative consultants; you have to learn to create an innovative culture organically within your company. That is the only way the core of your brand can be strategically connected to every product you make and service you provide.

This book is also about people who are at the heart of the innovation process. We mention two types of people throughout this book: those who purchase and/or use the product or service, and those in companies who are the innovative developers of the products and services. We include scenarios about the users throughout this book to provide a context for each chapter. The scenarios that start these chapters are fictitious. A common practice used in the early phase of development of new products and services, scenarios are often composites that represent critical aspects of the lifestyle tendencies of the intended market. The second type of people referred to are people in companies, and all of these people that we describe in our chapters are real. They have been extremely helpful and supportive in letting us find out what makes them tick and what enables them to become one of the new breed of innovators. We have worked with them in developing many of the case studies throughout this book.

This book is written to help you leverage your ability to find a way to thrive in the complex world we find ourselves in. As the often-used quote from Dickens' *A Tale of Two Cities* states, it is the best of times and the worst of times. The side of the coin you choose depends on how effective you are at turning obstacles into opportunities. You cannot plan for the future with the hope of always being lucky to succeed, but you can learn to always take full advantage of opportunities when you see them and increase the odds of success. As you look to the future and account for global economic and societal change, innovation is not everything; it is the *only* thing. Innovate or perish. Or, even worse, innovate or struggle to survive in the ever-tightening downward spiral toward cost-focused commoditization. Because there can be only one cheapest provider, no other choice is left.

This book is written in the sequence we would like you to read it, but each chapter stands on its own for the most part. We strongly suggest reading Chapters 1 through 3 before you roam. Chapter 1, "The New Breed of Innovator," talks about the new type of innovator, highlighting three outstanding leaders of innovation and aspects of their approach that anyone can use. Chapter 2, "Pragmatic Innovation—The New Mandate," argues that reliance on quality of manufacture initiatives can no longer be your buoy of survival; instead, innovation is the only approach to differentiation. Chapter 3, "The Art and Science of Business," gives a brief overview of the process of innovation and provides a context for understanding how to make it work for you.

The rest of the chapters discuss various aspects of the innovation process. Chapter 4, "Identifying Today's Trends for Tomorrow's Innovations," talks about reading trends and converting them into product and service opportunities. Chapter 5, "Design for Desire— The New Product Prescription," argues that innovation is about meeting people's desires, about fulfilling their fantasies. Chapter 6, "The Powers of Stakeholders—People Fueling Innovation," presents a new approach to analyzing all the stakeholders who affect or are affected by a product or service, a technique we call a Powers of 10 analysis. Chapter 7, "B-to-B Innovation—The New Frontier of Fantasy," argues that the business-to-business world is ripe for fantasy-driven innovation, and that a corporate strategic plan must connect the company to its brand and product.

Chapter 8, "Making Decisions for Profit—Success Emerging from Chaos," highlights the complexity of making decisions during the process of product development. Chapter 9, "A Process for Product Innovation," then highlights the detailed process focused on the earliest stages of product development, where innovation takes place. Chapter 10, "Creating a Blanket of IP to Protect Your Brand from the Elements," follows with a discussion of how to protect innovation and develop brands through the intellectual property system. Chapter 11, "To Hire Consultants or Build Internally—That Is the Question," helps you think about developing in-house innovation groups and complementing internal innovation with external consulting. Finally, the epilogue looks at the power of innovation through people and the opportunities they create.

We begin Chapter 1 with three people who manage large organizations and who have consistently produced innovative solutions in challenging and highly competitive markets. These individuals set the tone and provide the foundation of this book because each exemplifies the attributes of the new breed of innovator. As these three evolved in their professional careers, they connected their vocations and avocations to form a broader view—both of what was presently going on and of what was possible in the companies where they worked. As they developed, they were able to balance creative approaches with practical methods and to understand how to balance cost with a vision of how innovation could increase profits. Through a combination of education, personal ability, and effective partnerships, these three evolved into the role of the new breed of innovator, having established and managed environments for pragmatic innovation.

ACKNOWLEDGMENTS

As with any major endeavor, there are many people to thank for their input to this book and our thinking about this work.

Particular recognition and thanks go out to Keith H. Hammonds, Deputy Editor of *Fast Company*, for taking the time and interest to write the Foreword for this book.

Many people in the companies we write about have spent many hours speaking with us about their work and ideas. In order of appearance in this book, these include Dee Kapur of International Truck and Engine, Chuck Jones of Whirlpool, Edith Harmon and Josh Kaplan of New Balance, Astro Teller and Chris Kasabach of BodyMedia, Stephen Pierpoint of Adidas, Scott Charon and Gabe Wing of Herman Miller, Paul Basar of Lubrizol, Eric Close of RedZone Robotics, Bob Schwartz of Procter & Gamble, James Kyper of Kirkpatrick and Lockhart, Bruce Nussbaum of *Business Week*, David Kelley of IDEO, and Elizabeth Lewis of Product Insight.

Many students have worked with us in developing this work. These include Hillary Carey, Mark Hamblin, Harlan Weber, and Erika Wetzel. John Bellinger, Nathan Goldbatt, Rachel Lin, and James Raskob developed the quick-change machine tool interface mentioned in Chapter 7. Joshua Aderholt, Jeremy Canceko, Courtney Chu, Luke Hagan, Patrick Marcotte, Seth Orsborn, and Lisa Tsui developed the intelligent insole discussed in Chapter 9.

We are grateful to Jeff Calhoun of VistaLabs for his detailed comments on this manuscript and the ideas behind it. We also thank Anne Akay for her comments on this book and Stephen Boatwright for his comments on selected chapters.

We are indebted to our editor, Jim Boyd of Prentice Hall, who has made this process as seamless and as easy as possible. His encouragement and support throughout are deeply appreciated.

Several colleagues at Carnegie Mellon have provided inspiration and support. Professor Laurie Weingart of the Tepper School of Business has been our partner in teaching the Integrated Product Development course and has worked with us on several research projects. Ilker Baybars and Ken Dunn of the Tepper School of Business, Adnan Akay of Mechanical Engineering, Pradeep Khosla of the College of Engineering, and Dan Boyarski of the School of Design have been active supporters of our effort and proponents of our course.

We would also like to thank the illustrator, Shane Machir, for the artwork. Additional artwork, by Lisa Troutman.

1

THE NEW BREED OF INNOVATOR

Innovation is about people. Companies focus on customer needs, wants, and desires as they design new products; after all, products are purchased by and for those who will use them. Those who design the products also are people—ordinary people who apply their skills to develop new ideas and products. Yet certain individuals have evolved to a level of innovator who envisions, leads, and manages the complete context of a product or service. These people are the new breed of innovator, and they are the model for all of us to follow. Who are these innovators of today, how did they acquire the insight to innovate products that excite consumers, and how do they simultaneously inspire and motivate the people with whom they work? In this chapter we introduce three of these innovators in order to reveal their mentality and methods.

The New Breed of Innovator: Pragmatic Business

At the age of 18, Dee Kapur left India and arrived in New York City on the first leg of his journey to California to attend Stanford University. His flight was late, and he missed his connecting flight; Kapur found himself stranded in the Big Apple with $200, his suitcase, his tennis racquet, and little sense of what to do. He eventually got to Stanford, and although economically poorer, he gained a new sense of confidence. With no money to his name, he found that he had to be innovative in small ways every day just to make ends meet. His current drive for innovation in business has its roots in such experiences, when he had to seek new and efficient solutions in daunting circumstances.

After earning a degree in mechanical engineering from Stanford and his MBA at Carnegie Mellon, Kapur eventually landed at Ford Motor Company. At Ford, he continued to seek innovative ways to turn supposed barriers into opportunities. At one point, he ran the most profitable line of vehicles in the United States and was part of the group at Ford that helped transform the SUV and a pickup truck from a service vehicle into a lifestyle vehicle. In 2003, after a successful career at Ford, Kapur was named president of the Truck Division of International Truck and Engine.

Kapur believes in what he refers to as *pragmatic innovation*, a term that perfectly captures the balance between creativity and profit. He recognizes that, even as he leads an organization, he cannot mandate innovation. However, he can institute a management process that fosters it. Kapur models his approach to his employees with one dose inspiration and one dose instruction. The level of interpersonal relationships is reinforced by the practical, by budget allocations, and by reward and recognition. In his work with others and in his business procedures, Kapur holds up innovation as a clear signpost that shows the direction of his leadership. How you allocate your time and money and how you groom your employees show your priorities and establish incentives within a company. At the end of the day, Kapur keeps an eye on results. Although his upbringing and engineering training continuously ensure attention to facts, logic, and results, often the road to the outcome is newly laid. He likes to set targets for his company that he has "no freakin' idea how to get to." These targets are not just goals; they shape corporate culture. The targets create a demand for unconventional input, and, more often than not, they coalesce into a game plan that would not happen with a "safe" goal. In setting such goals, he has developed an instinct for finding the sweet spot between the acceptable and the impossible. Setting the bar where he does helps motivate those under him and creates an environment of creativity. He also sets a positive example by walking the walk; he strives to be the ideal he wants others to be. He has a directness and honesty that you instantly respect. He wastes neither words nor time. He does not look to blame others; instead, he looks to accomplish goals. He never seeks to embarrass people, and he knows the power of win-win.

Throughout his career Kapur has looked to identify the people who, like him, are looking at the broader picture. He realizes that you can never bring everyone along with total conviction, but if you build a core team right away, you can change the way a group or project team works. In any organization, he says, approximately 30 percent of the people are passionate about wanting to win or at least make a difference. The leader's challenge is to identify those people, groom them, harness their energy, and let them be a beacon for others. If one can garner the allegiance of that 30 percent, that is success. Spend time with the people who want to be motivated. Challenge and "jazz" them, and they will introduce a velocity and energy that will propel the rest along with them.

For Kapur, pragmatic innovation requires a balance of the left and right brain working in unison. Such a balance enables him to see situations in a broader way than many others. He can manage the duality inherent in complex corporate decision making. He intuitively understands the concept of moving from one level of viewing the problem to another. He attributes this in part to the fact that he not only has an analytical ability to understand engineering and business systems, but he also has a feel for the lifestyle side of products, he appreciates the human reaction, and he recognizes the compulsion that drives prospective buyers. He was raised in the Himalayas in India, but he also spent time in Europe when his father was transferred there in the course of his career. He has a global perspective born of his personal life: high school in the Himalayas, several years in Europe as a child, and an exposure to life's possibilities without the luxuries of coddling.

His ability to see the value of the different major players in the process enables him to manage and motivate others and to unify them toward common goals. It is not who is right or wrong, but what needs to be done to get to the next level. In our work with the auto industry, we saw many examples of managers who were loyal to their area of expertise and defensive about the requests for change or perspectives offered by other areas in the company. Many complain that employees in other areas of the company are myopic. If only they could learn to see the situation from another's perspective, they could move faster and make the right decision. Design stylists complain that others fail to grasp the gestalt, or entirety, of a design; when non-designers pick it apart and make changes to the pieces, they compromise the overall effect. Engineers argue about cost overruns and the inability to deliver on style without compromising performance quality. Manufacturing argues about the feasibility of maintaining tolerances given form complexity or material choices. Human factors and safety specialists constantly call for changes in engineering and styling to ensure a higher degree of safety. Cars are designed to be driven, but human-factors specialists are trained to think about when the car will fail. Marketing argues for details that stylists reject as incompatible with the new approach to style. In short, there are plenty of reasons to disagree. Kapur does not like to take sides; when he must, however, it is to ensure a successful outcome, and he strives to bring his team along with him. A persistent operating theme for him is "integrated execution!"

When Kapur started in automotive design, he was as fascinated with styling as he was with engineering. While directing the Truck Division at Ford, Kapur, along with marketeers Bob Masone and Allison Howitt and head truck designer Pat Schiavone, was viewing an old two-seat roadster with saddle leather interior. The car exuded high class, and at the same time, the leather reminded him of the saddles cowboys used. And those cowboys happen to be customers of pickup trucks. Wouldn't it be great if a pickup had a similarly luxurious interior, one that still connected to the cowboy aura? That leap led to the development of a limited-edition F-150 pickup with saddle leather interior, co-branded with the King Ranch in South Texas. The King Ranch accomplished a number of things inside Ford as well as with the F-150. The project not only made a strong brand statement of innovation for Ford, it also created a great working relationship with the whole team. Trucks and SUVs became the place where everyone wanted to be; it was where the action was. The new line of F-150s introduced in 2004 (and further discussed in the next chapter) was a product of the team that brought you the King Ranch as well as the Harley Davidson F-150 (designed jointly by Gordon Platto and Willie G. Davidson himself). According to Kapur, "The name of the game is to continually change it." That is the focus of Kapur's view on innovation.

Yet Kapur's last assignment at Ford was to deal with the challenging problem of controlling costs in vehicle programs. Controlling costs by itself is not a difficult task—cut out all unnecessary parts, and cheapen those that are integral. But that approach leaves the company with little to sell other than a low price. The challenge is to produce great products while meeting cost goals. More managers are needed who can handle both the creative innovation such as that in the King Ranch and the pragmatics of cost, because the combination of these two positions gives Kapur the ying and yang of what it takes to develop innovative products. Now, Kapur will see whether that same approach can help clarify and rebuild the International brand in the trucking industry.

Kapur sums up his approach to managing innovation in three steps:

1. Make innovation and boldness part of the culture—everyone needs to know what you stand for.

2. Role-model innovation as often and in as many forums as you can.

3. Institute a management process that fosters innovation.

Kapur lives by the vision that "the future for society and the country is vibrancy in innovation." Kapur is a new breed of innovator.

The New Breed of Innovator: Global Brand and Industrial Design

It was August, and Chuck Jones was at Michigan International Speedway competing in a vintage Indy car race. Jones started racing cars at the rather young age of 8, turned professional at age 15, and now—in addition to his career as vice president of global consumer design for the world's largest appliance manufacturer, Whirlpool Corporation—at age 44, he still keeps sharp by participating in a half dozen high-speed races each year. Driving at speeds of 168 mph requires a level of concentration that anyone could learn from, and Jones excels at it...he is still winning regional championships against competitors less than half his age. Jones considers this experience to be the kind of event that allows him to escape from the daily grind and keep things in perspective. He learned how to manage quality programs when working at Xerox Corporation, programs that were a major part of the Xerox success story of the 1980s. At Xerox, he directed several successful product programs for new copiers, and he came away with a thorough understanding of digital product interface. The discontinuities between his day job and hobby are very much how he views innovation—the ability to arrive at discontinuous solutions that yield paradigm shifts in your product, service, and brand.

Although Jones's formal degrees are in industrial design and human-factors engineering, his first degree was really from the fields in Indiana, where he grew up in farm country. He knows all about machines and how to disassemble and fix an engine. As a side note, Jones family lore has it that Chuck successfully diagnosed a problem on an engine, disassembled it, reassembled it, and got the engine running at age 5. On the farm, innovation meant having to find a fix for a broken gear on the combine during harvesting season at 4 A.M. when no stores were open. Discontinuity meant working on the family farm at 4 A.M. during harvest season when running the farm was just a family hobby and your dad had a day job as a chemical engineer. Tending to a hobby farm at 4 A.M. as a kid built a strong work ethic and solid values.

Although he trained primarily in industrial design, Jones, like Kapur, has balanced capabilities in the left and right parts of his brain. His engineering side is comfortable with the precision and logic of math, which has enabled him to thrive in management; at the same time, he explores the possibilities of creation through design. After finishing college, he gained experience in business and quality systems development. He went through several product development cycles at Xerox and had developmental jobs such as running the business strategy office, eventually becoming the manager of industrial design and human interface. Whirlpool recruited him, and he now directs one of the biggest global brand design, user interface, and consumer understanding programs in the world. From the headquarters of little-known Benton Harbor, Michigan, he manages the global design empires of the Whirlpool and KitchenAid product lines in the United States as well as the 11 other Whirlpool global brands, and he manages design for appliances under the Kenmore and IKEA brands.

One brand innovation championed by Jones and a team inside Whirlpool's North America business unit is the Gladiator GarageWorks line of products for garage and basement storage systems. The innovation team that developed the idea of Gladiator GarageWorks recognized that, in many households, women tend to take the lead for purchase decisions in every "living quarters" room— the kitchen, living room, bedrooms, bath. Therefore, the last bastions for men in the home are the basement and garage. With the Gladiator GarageWorks system, consumers may pay up to $25,000 extra when building or refurbishing a house for the sake of a "dream" garage shop, complete with quality shelving and cabinetry, a "Freezerator" that allows one to adjust the percentage used for refrigeration versus freezing, and a "Beverage Box" to keep 170 cold ones. The appliances sense both hot and cold temperature extremes; they not only refrigerate, they also have built-in heaters, ensuring that the contents stay chilled in a steamy hot garage but are never frozen in an unheated one. This new Whirlpool brand brought in $25 million in revenue in just its second year!

Jones's timing in going to Whirlpool was perfect. He had just gained experience in a company that went from being a "copier company" to a "document company." Xerox was in the printing business and making some of the most complex modern industrial and business printers in the world. The company was attempting to integrate complex digital-driven products with electronic, electromechanical, and mechanical systems in one product. The daily use of these machines is intense, and the complexity of interaction and range of users demanded an entirely new approach to the design of the interface of the products. Jones learned the power of digital interface design to connect people to machines. The best copier or printer in the world is useless if you cannot understand how to use it and if you waste more time making mistakes than the copies you want.

Jones understood that the appliance industry was ripe for the same change. He recognized that an appliance company could dominate in the industry if it could figure out how to improve the function and service without making the product interface too complex. He also knew that most appliance companies were still living in the "big white box" world without grasping the fact that the market had changed. Kitchens and laundry rooms were taking on a whole different meaning in the contemporary United States home. The washer and dryer were seen as a bland and generic commodity—a "sea of white," as Jones likes to call it. The old paradigm was that no one cared about the aesthetics of the laundry room—when one machine broke, you bought any other one, and possibly from the same brand. Only 18 percent of washers and dryers were sold as pairs.

So Jones leveraged the international structure of his group and, along with global engineering and brand marketing in Europe and the United States, helped create the Duet washer/dryer. The Duet adapted a technology platform from Europe to the tastes and reliability expectations of North America. The focus on consumer interaction and ergonomics led to the insight that the washer and dryer should be raised on a pedestal so that consumers do not have to bend over to reach inside the machines. The aesthetic and ergonomic statement of Duet has changed the face of laundry rooms. Today, more than 90 percent of Duets are sold in washer/dryer pairs. The product is so successful that Whirlpool was able to raise the price three times after its initial introduction. Each Duet machine sells for three times the average competitive machine because of its integrated consumer benefit package of world-class aesthetics, great energy efficiency, and benchmark ergonomics. Consumers see the value, and that is successful innovation!

While the Whirlpool brand has been enjoying tremendous success, there is an equally interesting story in Jones's developments in KitchenAid (another brand of Whirlpool Corporation). The KitchenAid mixer is an icon of the American kitchen and stands head and shoulders above the competition in perceived value. In the age of digital-driven products, the KitchenAid mixer stands alone as a throwback electromechanical marvel. Timeless like any great icon, it sits supreme in a kitchen of baby boomers or newlyweds. Often the anchor gift for a young couple's new kitchen, the mixer will last them until retirement. That's the good news.

The bad news is you cannot sell a lot of products if each lasts a lifetime—that is, unless you can leverage the brand equity, which KitchenAid has done with its new Pro Line series of countertop products. If you go to the nearest Williams-Sonoma store in the United States, you will see a line of products that are all in a neutral, metallic gray. They look like scale models of little factories and embody the heft and robust nature of the KitchenAid stand mixer. These are serious, professional-looking products. This new line is the interaction of organic growth and consulting at its best, designed by the in-house KitchenAid Brand Design Studio with support from Ziba, one of the world's best design consulting firms. The new line of gray KitchenAid children sits right next to the proud mixer parents, which come in a range of colors and finishes. The offspring are contemporary but bear a striking family resemblance both in appearance and in their iconic potential. The price tag of many of these new products is a mere $300 plus tax. Williams-Sonoma signed an exclusive agreement for six months, and, during Christmas 2003, they could not stock them fast enough. Imagine paying $300 for a waffle maker, which in the Pro Line series is not a waffle "iron" but a waffle "baker." On display nearby is a European waffle maker that sells for $50. Why would someone pay $300 for a waffle iron?

It is often the case that an experience on a vacation can become the stimulus for the purchase of a new product. For example, your kids may have loved the brunch at a Hilton because of the make-your-own-waffles experience with the large-scale professional-grade waffle iron. This big waffle iron has large handles that lock shut and allow the whole unit to be turned over, enabling users to make two waffles at a time. You walked the children through it the first time, and from then on, they were on their own. The machine steamed and hissed as the waffles cooked. The kids loved turning over that big handle and in a few minutes, out popped huge, thick waffles. Forget the muffins, Danishes, pancakes, and eggs. All the kids wanted to eat were waffles, and lots of them. Wouldn't it be great if you could give your kids the same experience in your home? Somehow the small, single-waffle iron no longer cut it. So when you got home from that vacation, you went to Williams-Sonoma, and there it was. Sitting next to the $50 Belgian waffle iron is the $300 KitchenAid waffle baker, just like the one that made the waffles the kids raved about on vacation. People buy SUVs for the experience of height, the roominess, the safety, and sometimes for all-wheel drive. These benefits are worth the extra fuel costs. Similarly, people buy KitchenAid for the experience; cost and size are thrown to the wind. Now Saturday can be a special family event as everyone relives a vacation experience.

What Jones (in a *Field of Dreams* scenario) knew and the team delivered on was that if they could make a compelling product that drafted off the success of KitchenAid, they would succeed—"If they built it, they would come"…and they would buy. The profit margins are enormous, more so than for many traditional Whirlpool products. Giving Williams-Sonoma a six-month exclusive for the new line added to its appeal and supported the price tag. The rest of the story is equally as interesting from a brand perspective. If you go into Target, you will see the same KitchenAid mixer (because this product crosses all demographics), but you will not see the Pro Line series. What you will see instead is a $50 set of KitchenAid products in Target red and individual KitchenAid tools selling for $20. This extension from upscale to box store is not easy to accomplish. Using the KitchenAid mixer as the anchor is an innovative marketing move that so far has paid huge dividends. The idea of updating and extending the brand of KitchenAid caught the competition napping.

Like Dee Kapur, Jones has learned to see the other perspectives in the company with equal clarity and respect. While he has a keen sense of visual design and style, he also knows the issues that impact the bottom line—the core business architecture. He and his Brand Studio directors oversee a group that includes industrial design, graphic design, interface design, user research, and human-factors engineering. His brand teams are multidisciplinary and work in an integrated way with other areas of the company.

Jones is one of the new breed of innovator. In five years, he has built his global brand group to more than 100 people from the 15 he started with, and his staff are all in demand from other brand- and consumer-driven companies that hope to hire them away and capture some of Whirlpool's success. When Jones was awarded the Smithsonian Institute's National Design Award at the White House in 2003, it was the culmination of his and his team's success of a multiyear strategy to make Whirlpool the most recognized appliance brand in the world and recognized as a design leader. Consistent with Kapur, Jones can "see" the playing field; that is, his experiences have enabled him to see and understand the interconnected challenges of design, engineering, and marketing.

As a leader of innovation, Jones has several main goals:

1. Make the resources—time, space, money—available for the team to explore; 20 to 30 percent of his resources goes to innovation.

2. Use the resources to keep a pipeline of innovation going; on a yearly basis, the group generates hundreds of ideas, explores dozens of the promising ones, and then focuses on a dozen as possible product or brand introductions.

3. Make the tough decisions on which ideas fit the corporate business case.

4. Create an environment where everyone has the opportunity to contribute; to build such a rich team of talent is meaningless unless you use that talent.

5. Track innovation, understand its impact, and make it visible throughout the company so that the value of the group is clear; what gets measured gets attention!

6. Hire people who embody both "book smarts" and "street smarts"—those who can use both sides of their brain.

The New Breed of Innovator: Engineering and Advanced Thinking

Edith Harmon's bachelor's and master's degrees are in mechanical engineering. But today, she heads one of the most dynamic advanced products groups in the clothing industry. Unlike a fashion company that makes shirts or jackets, New Balance makes state-of-the-art technology to support your body while you exercise. Athletic apparel, then, is more than fashion. It is materials, manufacturing, ergonomics, biomedical, and lifestyle all rolled into some clothes and a pair of shoes. Harmon was exposed to technology during a brief stint at GM followed by a career of designing aircraft engines at GE, and even a stint designing alternative power plants in a start-up in the 1980s. But she wanted to connect with consumers, and she wanted products with shorter life spans that she could follow from inception to market success. In the aircraft industry, you are lucky to see any real innovations, and one product literally lasts a lifetime.

With all of this engineering focus, how did she end up as the manager of future product concepts in what many see as a fashion-focused industry? Like Kapur and Jones, Harmon also has a well-tuned right brain to balance her engineering left brain. Raised in New York City, she grew up with strong exposure to and a love for the arts, with regular visits to museums and the theater. When she was an undergraduate engineering student, her favorite courses were art history and film. She gained an appreciation and respect for the more artistic people, an appreciation that she brought with her to her job at New Balance.

When you meet Harmon, you really aren't sure how to classify her; she fits none of the stereotypes of the engineer, designer, or business executive. Harmon meets the criteria for the new breed of innovator. She is a polyglot and can talk with equal comfort to designers, marketing, material engineers, and manufacturing. She is a skilled manager of the multiple disciplines needed to produce the new ideas developed in the advanced product concepts. Harmon fosters the kind of thinking that allows her team to balance creative possibilities with costs and production realities.

When Harmon hires someone to join her group, team dynamics is one of the main drivers. People need to respect each other. They need to balance each other; there should be no duplication in talents and effort, and each person's skills must be valued in the team. Each person must be self-motivated. Harmon sees her role as finding talented people who fit this mold and then giving them the environment and resources to excel.

Harmon encourages her team to try new ideas, as long as they fit in the larger business case of New Balance without the need to justify or defend them to the larger company. As a manager, she creates a buffer zone that protects her team and gives them freedom to explore. The goal is for the team to create fresh, usable ideas that balance aesthetic and functional appeal and that do not meet a preconceived notion—in other words, ideas that are innovative.

In managing the Advanced Products Group, Harmon focuses on the process rather than the end result. She gives her team the freedom to explore and meander within the process, the flexibility to obtain insights and findings that will direct their path to an end result. This freedom encourages self-motivation, a critical ingredient for innovation, and the process is a requirement to replace the lone inventor with the group innovator, who churns out a wealth of fresh, workable ideas. The group has balance, whereas the individual typically does not.

One of the many successes for Harmon's Advanced Products Group is the 1100 Ultra Trail Shoe. The shoe is a premium running shoe for trails, featuring waterproof, coated uppers, integral "scree" gaiters to prevent dust and pebbles from getting into the shoe, and rubberized toe bumpers to protect the toes. The outer sole looks almost like a tire tread, engineered for traction in rough terrain, protecting the sole from bruising, and allowing water to pour through the shoe (more on that in a minute).

The team embraced a user-centered design approach from start to finish. In developing the product, they focused on "ultra runners" who race for at least 50 miles and perhaps even 100 miles at a time. By meeting these runners' needs, the team knew that they would meet the needs of the average trail runner as well. The research was holistic, representing a range of stakeholders interviewed from race directors to the publisher of *UltraRunning* magazine—and, of course, ultra runners. Three different types of ultra runners were interviewed: "newbies" just getting into it, "veterans" to whom ultra running is the center of their lifestyle, and "elites" who are driven to win these grueling races and are often sponsored by shoe companies. Three of each type were interviewed in their homes, on the trail, and at races. The team spent many hours running with these folks and experiencing their world firsthand. To make sure they understood the needs of runners in all different terrains, they conducted studies of runners in places they couldn't get to, like Utah, Colorado, New Mexico, and Alaska. Here, they sent the runners disposable cameras for them to record their experiences, and then they conducted phone interviews using the images as a catalyst.

One interesting aspect of ultra running discovered by the team was that these runners intentionally run through streams. When running 100 miles, feet begin to burn and swell. Cool water is a way to refresh irritated feet. So Harmon's team wanted to both allow water in and then whisk it out. Near the toe is an open hydrophobic mesh that lets water in but dries quickly, while in the sole are "drain and dry" holes that open while a person is running to let the water back out.

The team also researched related sports, such as adventure racing and orienteering, and other lifestyle products that address related needs identified through their research. A business case was built, including branding and strategic research, understanding the competitor landscape, and determining how to position and distribute the new product—namely, in specialty stores.

The team followed the type of process we discuss in Chapter 9, "A Process for Product Innovation." As soon as they understood the opportunity, they began extended brainstorming sessions followed by prototyping of the concepts. Any feasible concepts went immediately into usability testing. Many of the users they had interviewed tried the working prototypes and then gave the team feedback. After making further modifications, the team repeated the process until they had designed a great product.

This process is the ideal product development process. Few teams in practice are given the resources and support to follow such a complete, user-driven design process. But the results speak for themselves. The shoe was awarded a gold award from Running Network, and sales have been at about 10,000 pairs per year—quite good for a specialty product like the 1100 Ultra. It takes a manager like Harmon to develop and support a team and environment for this approach toward innovation and developing new products.

As a manager of the Advanced Products Group, Harmon's goals include the following:

1. Make resources available—not just time and money, but also the freedom to fail.

2. Create innovation groups of individuals, each of whom has some distinct skills to bring to the table, so that the value of each person's ideas contributes to mutual respect within the groups.

3. Foster self-motivation within the groups to encourage enthusiastic participation stemming from belief in and enjoyment of the process and goals.

So Who Are the New Breed of Innovators?

Edith Harmon, Chuck Jones, and Dee Kapur are the new breed of innovators. They have achieved a pragmatic sense of balance between the pressing needs of business and the open-ended possibilities of product opportunities. They also balance the corporate strategic big picture with the needs of particular product programs. It is more than using a different set of methods; they have a different state of mind that they bring to every decision they make. They have acquired this state of mind; they have learned how to manage a process for innovation and how to cultivate people to succeed in that process. It is a mentality and understanding that you also can learn. We introduce you to these individuals so that you can learn from them. The question to ask yourself is this: What can you do now to become an effective pragmatic innovator?

They have become respected in their companies, even though their approaches are not typical, because they understand how to foster and manage a corporate environment of innovation in companies such as Ford, Whirlpool, and New Balance. Although these three innovators are all in larger companies, innovators exist in every type and size of company. The next chapter describes the young and the restless team from start-up BodyMedia, and later in this book, you will read the case study of Eric Close, president and CEO of RedZone Robotics. In contrast, these individuals have made pragmatic innovation work in small start-up companies. This book also discusses David Kelley of IDEO and others in product-development consulting firms.

These individuals know that innovation is all about people, from the team who develops the product to the customers who use it. They know how to identify motivated and skilled people with whom to work and that innovation is about succeeding with others and learning how to set goals. These leaders are comfortable with and often enjoy the challenge of finding innovative solutions in seemingly contradictory situations. Where others see risk, they see opportunity. Their managing style is reminiscent of hockey great Wayne Gretzky's style of playing (when he was still playing): Instead of skating to where the puck was, he skated to where the puck would be.

Innovation Revealed

This book is about people. It is about the innovators who envision and create new products and services for the new global economy. It is also about the people who demand innovation at home, work, and play; in other words, it is about you. Throughout this book are many case studies about people and companies that innovate solutions for the consumer and the business-to-business world. These people and case studies are real, many taken from our consulting, research, and educational initiatives—people like Kapur and Jones and Harmon. But also throughout this book, especially at the beginning of many chapters, are stories about users of these products. Because innovation is about understanding the needs, wants, and desires of those people who affect the success of the product in the marketplace, scenarios of these people are a critical tool in the practice of innovative product development. These scenarios are developed by product developers to provide product-use context. Although they are projections of real people, these stories of end users are not real.

This book is also about the process of innovation. It is not about managing new products after the fact, where a new product created elsewhere in the company now requires strategic marketing. It is not about the traditional business topics that fall under the label of innovation management. It is about the business of innovating—the business of finding opportunities in the marketplace and of developing products to achieve those opportunities. The tools, methods, and insights discussed result from our consulting and research projects. These are the tools of the new breed of innovator.

The result is a step-by-step guide to help you through the innovation process. It is not, however, a set of mindless instructions, a checklist that will do the work for you. Innovation requires thought. You, the reader of this book, can excel at it if you take the time to think about the context of the world around you. If you are looking for a way to reshape the way you lead, direct, manage, think, and practice, this book helps you learn how to fish in the seas of opportunity that exist in the interconnected new global economy. If you are someone who just wants to view the excitement of innovation up close, to understand what it takes to create a great product and deliver it to your door, this book gives you front-row insight into great companies, processes, people, and ideas in product and service development today.

2

PRAGMATIC INNOVATION— THE NEW MANDATE

As companies struggle to look for ways to compete against low-margin overseas competitors, they must turn to their creative side because cost-cutting manufacturing and quality initiatives no longer provide the competitive edge. Differentiation now must happen through innovation; that is the strategic weapon that drives profit in the new global economy.

Burlington, VT. Robert Nicholson was not really concerned about the health of his heart when he went in for his annual physical. Although his dad had died of a heart attack, Rob figured he was reasonably healthy at 46. He worked out a few times a week and, although he did have a soft spot for pepperoni pizza, he usually watched what he ate. So he was particularly shocked when he found out that his cholesterol count and blood pressure had risen over the past year. His physician seemed concerned as well, which is why he put Rob on a 24/7 continuous health-monitoring system. Because Rob imagined and dreaded the hassle of wearing a monitor, he was pleasantly surprised to see and feel the SenseWear armband that held the sleek little monitor by BodyMedia. The system continuously monitored his relevant vital functions and then downloaded them to his computer. The software then tracked his health with the promise of telling him to call his doctor if anything looked awry. But the biggest surprise was that he found himself showing off the little monitor to all his friends. This was the first body monitor he heard of that could really become a part of your life.

A Mandate for Change

In their struggle to adapt to the new forces affecting the development of emerging products and services, executives of many companies find themselves "drinking from a fire hose." These managers are thirsty for answers but find it hard to handle all that is streaming at them: the volume of opportunities and demands, of ideas and constraints, of potential directions and hurdles. The pressures of external competition, of internal management issues, and of financial hurdles are overwhelming. These often result in analysis paralysis and a lack of insight into where to proceed, leaving one trying to put out daily fires instead of working productively toward larger goals. Managers and VPs have been accustomed to being part of companies that buy and sell divisions and, in a sense, to being bought and sold themselves. As a result, they have constantly been under new CEO leadership and often have been required to move semiannually to newly acquired divisions, where their assignment is to obtain unrealistic results in the new environment with new personnel.

Executives have been handed a new mandate: Grow the business using innovation, and do it organically using the company's existing resources, outsourcing only as needed. If that is not enough, they have been told they cannot compromise on manufacturing quality. Now that salary raises and career advancement are based on staying in one place long enough to establish cycles of innovation, managers are challenged to find methods and tools that are replicable and that connect to corporate strategy to grow market share and brand loyalty.

Pragmatic Innovation (and How It Differs from Invention)

One of the key concepts to understand is how innovation today differs from invention and why innovation in business must be pragmatic. When Thomas Edison developed the system of electrification and the electric light bulb, and when Ford perfected the assembly line to produce an affordable automobile, the Model T, those were inventions. One replaced gas as the primary energy for lighting at work and at home, and the other made gas (fossil fuel)-driven vehicles as inexpensive as horses and horse-drawn carriages. What was formerly beyond the imaginative daydream of the common person became an essential part of new routines and enhanced lifestyles. These inventions were technological leaps. The scale of the leaps was significant in one dimension but lacking in others. The Model T was noisy, uncomfortable, and dangerous to start, and early electric light was not as warm and attractive as gaslight or candles. We are at a point in the evolution of technology where inventions are still occurring, but innovation has replaced invention as the main day-to-day driving force in the global economy.

It is common for a word to shift in meaning to reflect changes that are occurring in business or the world at large. The term *innovation* is now being used to describe a new force in business in the same way the word *quality* shifted in emphasis and in meaning in the last two decades of the twentieth century. What we mean by innovation extends beyond invention of new technology and includes a thoughtful and insightful application, delivery, extension, or recombination of existing technology. Although innovation might involve a big engineering leap of technological invention, innovation may simply be technologically incremental. The key is that an innovation is a valued leap from the viewpoint of consumers whether or not it is incremental from the producer's standpoint.

Innovation, then, is a new comprehensive approach to product and service development that scores high on consumer value, connecting to and altering consumer lifestyles. Innovation is the ability to find nonobvious opportunity in what, after the fact, seems obvious and needed to everyone else. It is the ability to see extraordinary potential in ordinary events. It is the ability to see how to fulfill the desire of others, to elevate their common, everyday world into uncommon lifestyle experiences. We have further clarified the term *innovation* by adding the word *pragmatic*. Pragmatic innovation is a balanced approach that not only explores a range of interesting alternatives but converts that exploration into successful, profitable products. Pragmatic innovation is a process of inspired management of diverse teams working on a significant opportunity in the market. We use the term *pragmatic innovation* and *innovation* interchangeably throughout this book.

Whereas everyone can be innovative in addressing the problems in his or her own personal life, managing innovation in a corporate context is a more complex challenge. In business, innovation must be not only the development of products or services that are useful, useable, and desirable, but it also must be marketable and profitable. Balancing new insights with the practical realities of the marketplace requires a balance of vision and business acumen. Finding the right pH value between a product that is too acidic for the public to digest and one that is too basic to generate appeal is the challenge that companies face. The stakes are significant, but so are the profits. The point is that "basic" commodity products will not generate significant profit. Companies often choose the basic option because they see the opposite as dangerous, that developing "acidic" products might be trendy but too costly to risk without a clear return on profit. Instead, finding the balanced approach of pragmatic innovation will grow the company and keep it competitive in today's global economy.

A great example of innovation with minimal technological advances is the redesign of a pager by Motorola in the 1990s that had few enhanced features but offered colorful faceplates. Based on the faceplates alone, Motorola was able to successfully charge an extra $15 per unit.[1] Or consider the design of the Palm V, a commercially important advancement in the generations of Palm PDA devices. IDEO designed the unit for Palm. According to Tom Kelley, general manager of IDEO, the Palm V was designed with essentially the same technology as the previous-generation Palm but was aesthetically and ergonomically designed to appeal to executives and to women in general. The device was given organic lines, made thinner, and finished with brushed aluminum. The product was successfully sold at an additional $150 and expanded the PDA market.[2]

Invention is often the output of an individual genius, and inventions also come out of groups dedicated to an objective that results in a superior technological advance. The focus in invention is on the device more than the experience. Inventors are happy with Rube Goldberg solutions that work, failing to see the value in ergonomics

---

1 Postrel V. I. *The Substance of Style: How the Rise of Aesthetic Value Is Remaking Commerce, Culture, and Consciousness*. HarperCollins, New York, 2003. p. 67.

2 *The InnRoad*. A film produced by R. Lambert and presented by Advanced Elostomer Systems, 2004.

and aesthetics. Innovation is customer-driven, a carefully crafted integrated response to customer needs and desires. It must be broader in scope to take into account the myriad of factors that make products successful. Starbucks did not invent coffee; it changed the way you experience it. Starbucks took a risk pushing the quality of the taste of coffee, the feeling of the drinking environment. It charged a price that no one would have anticipated, but everyone was willing to shell out. Chrysler did not invent the PT Cruiser; it created an innovative retro-future interpretation of a hot rod, a small van and a station wagon, while simultaneously extending its established brand. General Motors took the Hummer and turned it into the ultimate statement of fashion and security and hit a post-9/11 emotional need to make the bulky and awkward into a trend. BodyMedia, as we will soon see, did not invent sensors to measure acceleration, heat flux, skin temperature, or skin response. Their innovation was to extend sensor technology into a contemporary-lifestyle wearable product with easy-to-interpret and up-to-the-minute personal health data being collected 24/7 regardless of the activity.

Invention has an important role in advancing society's abilities to meet demanding needs. Consider the technological challenge for fuel-cell technology, biodegradable materials, and nanotechnology to noninvasively perform surgery. But invention tends to be focused along the technology dimension only. The invention—the technology—is not enough. A successful product needs to consider the complete delivery of the technology as an object or service to be used, desired, and considered useful. In other words, the successful delivery of a new technology requires innovation.

Invention and discovery must continue. We do not question the basic and core value of these two activities. The difference is that we are now talking about pragmatic innovation rather than applied technology and invention. Pragmatic innovation requires observation, interpretation, and cycles of prototyping comprehensive versions of intended solutions, not only of technology. This is as true in consumer products, the medical industry, and business-to-business. The other important concept of today's innovator is that he or she is customer-driven, not invention-driven. Finding what customers want and developing innovative solutions often means that you must bring new capabilities to a company to meet emerging customer needs. It also means that the company is not defined by its history of invention or by the number of utility patents it owns. The company's core is its knowledge of the customer and its capability to meet customer needs.

Pragmatic innovation is driven by and must respond to three factors: social change, economic situations, and technical advances. Each opportunity for a new product arises due to different combinations of changes in these factors. The social dimension is especially interesting. Responding to changes in trends and developing solutions that meet those trends tends to be the most successful strategy from a brand standpoint and allows for fat profit margins. The Segway is a great technological solution for personal transport, but the company failed to predict the lack of societal acceptance. The Prius, introduced by Toyota, anticipated the growing acceptance of hybrid power magnified by an increase in gasoline prices. Whereas both Honda and Toyota made initial hybrid versions that were met with mixed results, Toyota stuck with it and found a breakthrough solution.

Developing innovative products is not easy. The challenge now is not inventing and rushing new unrefined technology into the marketplace. The challenge is to provide more integrated, holistic solutions that address consumer needs, products, and services that respond to the changes in social conditions, economics, and technology. Given consumer expectations at home and at work, a product must successfully maximize its core technology, have a clear use in daily life, be easy to use, and be attractive enough to appeal to sensory desires. Many companies have been trying to compete by being excellent in one or two of these categories. We fully recognize the challenge in optimizing all these categories, but it is the level required for effective global competition and the core to achieving successful innovation. To be an innovative company, everyone must contribute in his or her own way to changing the culture and creating an environment that generates true consumer value.

Everybody, in some way, is an innovator at either work or home. Companies need to help their employees turn their innovation abilities, often focused on their avocation at home, into innovation in their vocation. Almost every way that you find to improve upon a task is an innovation. You may have found the perfect way to save time getting to work. You may have a unique strategy for raking leaves or for shoveling snow. It may be that you find yourself pressed for time and are preparing the same meal over and over, such as macaroni and cheese. Sometimes, you just open a package of the Kraft mix, that blue box sitting in everyone's pantry. But at other times, you might cook it from scratch. It's pretty easy. You boil the elbow noodles. Mix in some melted butter, milk, shredded cheddar. Sprinkle with breadcrumbs, and bake. You might experiment a bit by changing the pasta to penne and adding a dash of mustard and Worcestershire sauce. Each change is an innovation, a modification, or extension from the original. Not every example of personal innovation converts into a profitable idea, and some of the innovative ideas that work best for you might be rejected even by your family. When making a meal, you can afford to have some ideas that work and some that do not. When companies innovate and fail, the price is much higher and the factors that dictate success and failure are far more complex. The process of experimentation to find the right solution, however, is fundamentally the same. You can be the average Joe making adjustments to improve your car in your garage, or Steve Jobs inventing the personal computer industry in his.

How do you instill that feeling of risk and experimentation in employees in a 100-year-old company with publicly traded stock in a mature industry with global competitors aimed at defeating you in every market segment in which you compete? When you do get that new insight, how do you translate it into a useful, useable, and desirable solution that will be produced flawlessly, distributed, and sold in a systematic and thoughtful way in an appropriate amount of time to be ahead of your competition? If that is not enough, your solution has to stay competitive long enough to generate a return on investment and contribute to the company's well-established reputation for excellence. This is exactly what Dee Kapur was faced with when he started the program to develop the 2004 Ford F-150.

Moving from Invention to Innovation at Ford: The Redesign of the F-150

The Model T was an invention that made the automobile accessible to the middle-class, mostly male, consumer 100 years ago. The recent trend in the pickup industry, which is both male- and female-driven across many economic segments, required an innovative solution that would reestablish the F-150 as the undisputed leader in the pickup truck market. The F-150 has been the best-selling vehicle in America since 1982, having sold almost 30 million units. In 2003 alone, 850,000 F-150s were sold. Every seven years or so, the company undertakes a major redesign of the vehicle. Because Ford makes a significant percentage of its profits on its wildly successful F-150, why should it mess with success? Why redesign it? Well, there are many reasons. Three main ones are Chevy, Chrysler, and Toyota, and a fourth is Nissan. Each of these competitors must adapt to changes in the marketplace. Industry styles change, and a vehicle begins to look dated. Lifestyle trends change, so the expectations of the customer base change with regard to features and performance. New technology becomes standard on vehicles and must be incorporated into the design. Manufacturing technology changes, requiring the design to change to maximize the effectiveness of the production capabilities. Regulations change, requiring new fuel-efficiency standards with new engine technologies and new use of materials to lighten the vehicle. Perhaps the most important change during the 1990s was that the truck as a workhorse evolved into the work and play stallion. The SUV lifestyle trend started to extend into the truck market.

Ford was being attacked by Chevy's more aggressive designs, Toyota's quality, and Chrysler's muscle theme with Ram trucks. If Nissan creates a more exciting and better-performing truck, which it has in its Titan, Ford loses market share and its core profit. So the product development team at Ford had to innovate to compete. If they failed, the company would lose its cash cow. If the team succeeded, however, they could regain market share and gain a significant part of the new number of buyers in that evolving truck segment (mostly upscale). The challenge was to develop an innovative approach to re-creating and extending the concept of "Ford Tough," and the solution was evident in the 2004 release of the F-150.

Ford designed models for five different market segments. Instead of relying on geographic, age, and income segmentation, Ford studied how F-150s were being used and created product user segments and scenarios. The base model F-150, the XL, is the basic workhorse for farm and construction. The STX is for a younger "wheels and tunes" crowd, those who customize their trucks and prefer certain features to be base-level and expendable. The XLT is for families, with the option of a spacious supercrew cab, complete with a full-size back door. It has all the functionality of a truck. At the same time, a two-car family does not have to compromise their ability to haul the kids, because the work truck is also a family mobile.

Kapur's team went beyond these three traditional truck markets and identified two additional segments. These segments were composed of people who buy trucks because they are cool and provide the fantasy of off-road driving and safety. The FX4 is for bragging rights, for those who want a truck that stands out. It has options that are not available on other models, such as the black leather interior complete with leather-wrapped steering wheel and chrome-clad floor shifter. Its flashy look weds truck strength with sports car style. The fifth model is a luxury truck, the Lariat, with an interior more closely related to a living room than to a vehicle. Although still a truck, it provides the essence of comfort, even having power-adjustable foot pedals so that the huge dude and the tiny wife can both call this truck theirs. The reality, however, is that this "pickup" truck will likely never stray from an asphalt road and never carry more than antiques and the family suitcases.

Dee Kapur, who is highlighted in Chapter 1, "The New Breed of Innovator," led the beginnings of the F-150 redesign. At a time when Ford had tarnished its "Quality Is Job 1" badge as a result of the Explorer tire fiasco, Kapur kept his eye on the challenge ahead of him. He was faced with maintaining the number-one position for the F-150, the center of profit for the company. He sheltered the team from the major external problems the company was facing and provided a forum for innovation. He supported the ambitious tiered-segment approach because of innovations he saw in the marketing research and analysis. Innovation resulted in both the external and interior aesthetic and feature design to create a distinctive new look. Kapur challenged engineering to meet the demands of the new design while maintaining a commitment to quality and craftsmanship. Kapur knew that the status quo was not good enough, and Ford retained its leadership in the small truck market with the introduction of the new line.

Although Ford did its homework to assess its customers' desires, even its own expectations have been exceeded. In the months following the new F-150's release, 57 percent of buyers bought the FX4 and Lariat versions of the pickup, models that have the highest profit margins, whereas Ford had expected that these premium models would account for only 40 percent of sales. Although automobile sales were slow in early 2004, the F-150 was on target to set a sales record.

On top of these five models, Ford maintained a flagship, signature vehicle that it created as a rolling advertisement for its brand. The market size was not as important as who purchased the truck and what statement they made with it. The King Ranch version of the F-150, mentioned in Chapter 1, has seats made from saddle leather. No two seats are identical in look, and owners are responsible for treating the leather as they would a saddle. Ford produces only 20,000 of these each year, but they meet a premium-priced market and enrich Ford's brand equity. Ford also chose to increase visibility and brand equity at the upper end of its pickup portfolio with a co-branded model with Harley Davidson. The Harley truck, designed in collaboration with Harley legend Willie G. Davidson, captures the look and feel of Harley's renowned bikes. These special models, the King Ranch truck and the Harley truck, are outcomes of insights based on extensive customer research, the result of an innovation process in which product developers became so familiar with real people that they could design those customers' dreams in truck form.

Innovation in Start-Ups

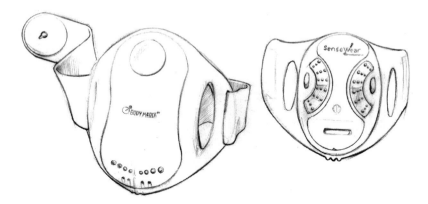

On the twelfth floor in a renovated office building at the foot of the Smithfield Street Bridge, a famous Pittsburgh, Pennsylvania, landmark built two centuries ago, sits an entrepreneurial high-tech start-up company that epitomizes the concept of innovation. The office space has won several awards for its novel use of low-cost materials and has the feel of an open landscape that characterizes the company's horizontal organization. White stretch fabric hangs from the ceiling in a dramatic way that shields but does not completely hide the exposed details of the original architecture. When the heating and cooling system kicks in, the fabric expands into large sails, giving the feeling of being on a sailing ship, an apt metaphor for the river below and the activity within. The atmosphere is creative but minimalist, and it is just the right mix to keep the mostly young interdisciplinary employees inspired. The views out the windows show a panoramic view of the confluence of the Allegheny and Monongahela Rivers, the point in Pittsburgh where the Ohio River is conceived. These are the same rivers that were used in the last Pittsburgh revolution. The once-polluted rivers that were filled with coal and slag barges are now a center of tourism and leisure boats. The new revolution is innovation.

The open space is filled with desks, laboratories, computers, and a prototyping studio that can build anything from high-end electronics to wearable product concepts; they even have professional sewing machines used in fashion design and manufacture. Bulletin boards appear throughout, filled with charts, pieces of the latest technology in materials, and images of people involved in all sorts of everyday activities. In the lobby, which melds with the desks of programmers, is a glass-top table with a box underneath filled with sand that you can reach into and play with, a remnant icon from Sandbox Advanced Development, the predecessor to BodyMedia.

In that space are also the some of the world's leading experts on body sensing, ergonomics of wearable devices, the analysis and mining of monitoring data, and cutting-edge aesthetics. BodyMedia, a small but growing biotechnology company, was founded by a foursome in 1999 with the mission to "be the recognized leader in integrated products and services that track and promote health and wellness through continuous body monitoring." CEO Astro Teller has an impressive lineage as the grandson of Edward Teller and of Gerard Debreu; Edward Teller was the father of the hydrogen bomb and advisor to six United States presidents, and Debreu was an economics Nobel Prize winner. Astro Teller has a Ph.D. in computer science and looks more like a rock star (with his below-shoulder-length hair, goatee, and mustache) than an executive. Another founder, CTO Ivo Stivoric, does not have an engineering degree. Neither does the VP of product design and mechanical development, Chris Kasabach. Instead, both have several degrees in industrial design. The fourth founder, Chris Pacione, VP of interaction design and marketing communications, does not have a marketing degree. Before teaming with Pacione and Teller, Stivoric and Kasabach had worked together in a research lab at Carnegie Mellon University developing five generations of wearable computers. Prior to returning to Pittsburgh to teach, where he ended up connecting with the other founders, Pacione had worked as an interface designer for one of the leading interaction design consulting firms in the world, Fitch. The team leads one of the most advanced and exciting technology companies in body health monitoring today.

Their product, the SenseWear armband body monitor, has won multiple national awards and has been featured in the *Wall Street Journal*, *Time*, and *Business Week*, among others. Against the odds in a climate of start-ups going bust, the company grew to 31 employees, raised $22 million in venture funding, and became a profitable company in its first five years. It has three significant utility patents issued on its core technology and nearly 50 more pending in the United States and abroad! The company also sells its products indirectly through partnerships that include Roche Diagnostics for clinical weight management and Apex Fitness as part of a weight-loss program and through resellers in the scientific research market.

The four founders represent further examples of the new breed of innovator. As an innovative team, they have developed a style of working that allows them to deliver state-of-the-art solutions to product opportunities. That working style incorporates interaction between their employees and their customers, a research and development approach, and a culture that keeps them on the cutting edge of discovery and application. For instance, SenseWear is not only an elegant monitoring device, it is also part of a complete service of interpreting the diverse streams of information generated by and stored within the device over periods as short as a few minutes or as long as a few weeks. BodyMedia's breakthrough insight into the need for a complete product and service solution occurred when the founders realized, after extensive observation and research with end users, that people want to incorporate the body monitoring into their everyday life (a product) and that both experts and novice users had a variety of potential applications for the information they monitored (a service). For instance, the SenseWear device might be used to accurately track calories burned during exercise, information that can be used in Web-based software (also provided by BodyMedia) that enables both personal trainers and their customers to track the success of a weight-loss regimen. Or the device might track vital cardiac signs for someone such as Rob Nicholson, mentioned previously in this chapter. The SenseWear combination of an elegant unobtrusive product, one with a simple and seamless download and easily understood interface, gave BodyMedia the right combination of innovative ideas to create a breakthrough in body monitoring.

Innovation can happen in both large and small companies. The nimble small companies, however, are often in a position to innovate without the bureaucracy and inertia of stability and the status quo. Large corporations have also found ways to build an entrepreneurial attitude, often by relying on small interdisciplinary advanced product development teams. But the new generation of start-ups is all about innovation, about change. BodyMedia developed its SenseWear product not because it had a technology looking for an application. Instead, the team had the training to observe societal trends. The team put forth the effort to understand the emergence of the desire for—and, in some cases, the need for—unobtrusive real-time monitoring of body performance. They were able to recognize this opportunity because they had extensive experience and expertise in wearability and computing.

The team of four founders at BodyMedia had gained experience in these areas through their education and experiences at Carnegie

Mellon University. The team was a spin-off of a research lab in the College of Engineering. The lab was focused on the fact the technology advances were allowing for the development of highly functional computers that could be carried or worn. Whereas most labs would have addressed size alone from a technology standpoint, this lab hired research assistants who had recently graduated from the university's department of industrial design. The team of Chris Kasabach and Ivo Stivoric started to produce much more comprehensive prototypes that included product semantics—the form and interface features that describe the aesthetics of the product, human factors, and market-driven aesthetics not found in most engineering-driven labs. The result was prototypes that looked and operated like mass-produced products. When designing wearable technology for military applications for equipment inspection, they took into account that most soldiers using the equipment were Game Boy-savvy and between the ages of 18 and 24. Their work attracted researchers at Intel, and they were asked to push the concept of usability and reduction of size to new areas of application. This project brought the entire team together as Astro Teller added a computer science dimension and Chris Pacione brought in communication and interface expertise. They also added new industrial design research assistants to the team— Francine Gemperle and David Aliberti.

The first prototype concept in the university setting was given the name Digital Ink. The idea was that your pen could also be your computer. The nice thing is that everyone carries and uses a pen, and building off that common tool would make everyone instantly comfortable with "computing." Although the concept was fantasy from the team's imagination, they had enough experience with technology to know this product was feasible, and enough practical understanding to create an innovative integration and delivery of technology in a product that everyone would embrace and that was eventually patented. The success of the product concept enabled the core team to spin out of Carnegie Mellon to start a consulting firm, Sandbox Advanced Development. The goal was to generate enough money consulting to start a new company where they would develop their own products. Within a year, they were on their way, and the original sandbox is in the lobby today, as mentioned earlier, as a reminder of where they have been and the attitude of free-flowing ideation they want to maintain.

Small and large companies alike need to build off of expertise. But innovation comes from trained insight and process. BodyMedia follows a rigorous process of innovation and exploration, processes that we discuss throughout this book. The result is a unique capability in the growing market of body monitoring.

The SenseWear device itself is comfortable and nonintrusive to wear, located at the optimal location of the body, balancing ergonomics and function. Rather than projecting a medical image, the device is a beautiful aesthetic. So it can be worn overtly rather than hidden. It is a statement of lifestyle rather than a banner of medical need. Its patented system analyzes body output such as total calories burned, duration of physical exercise, number of steps taken, active energy expenditure, and sleep onset and wake. The functional, ergonomic, aesthetic, and overall experiential qualities of the SenseWear redefined body monitoring in a market that had provided technology with little care for the experience of use.

Manufacturing Quality—The New Commodity

BodyMedia's success comes from a pragmatic approach to innovation. Any company producing a product or service that wants to differentiate, that wants to avoid being a commodity, must innovate. Innovation is the key to the competitive edge. That edge used to be found downstream in quality programs. Today, innovation is the theme that has replaced quality improvement in companies around the world. Not in the sense that quality programs are lessening in importance, but quality programs no longer offer a competitive advantage. Quality programs, such as Six Sigma, focus on producing zero-defect manufactured goods, where the goal is to improve the short-term and long-term hard-quality aspects of a product or delivery of a service. These methods have led to successful production of high-quality products, yielding goods that meet tolerance and other functional expectations, products that maintain that effectiveness throughout the life of the product. These quality methods have set a new standard; they have improved company processes and products so well that practically all companies now implement some kind of quality initiative. In fact, they must, because to be competitive everyone now must have high-quality manufacturing standards.

But now that quality manufacturing is simply the cost of doing business, corporate leaders have recognized their mandate to find other avenues for increasing bottom-line profits. Much recent effort has been directed at cost cutting. Wal-Mart's success has led many companies to see lower costs as an avenue for higher profits. Although Wal-Mart's no-nonsense price negotiations with suppliers are well known to the public, business leaders have been enticed more by Wal-Mart's cost-cutting improvements to the supply chain itself. Wal-Mart was a leader in implementing continuous replenishment programs and vendor-managed inventories, systems that have been critical to Wal-Mart's ability to keep costs down. Like quality programs, these business process enhancements are quickly becoming necessary standard operating procedures for every industry. But efficiency gains from these systems are showing up less and less in bottom-line profits and more and more in lower prices for consumers, which results in lower top-line revenues.

Attention is back on innovation as a way for top-line growth, now that companies are efficiently producing and supplying high-quality products and services. Quality programs had a guaranteed impact on the bottom line for those companies that were the first to adopt them. But after all competitors implement quality initiatives, quality programs no longer provide a competitive advantage. If they are not a competitive advantage, they are like a commodity, something every-one has. Microeconomics teaches that marginal profits are zero for commodities, that revenues simply cover the costs of wages, depreci-ation of equipment, and so on. Only those companies that are on the efficient cost frontier can continue to stay in business—anyone whose costs are too high must sell at a loss. Previously, when some compa-nies had higher quality to offer, they could sell at higher prices and afford higher costs. Now that quality manufacturing is accessible to all, quality differentials have shrunk, and higher costs are unafford-able. Offshoring is a result of firms' need to stay on the efficient fron-tier, the need to keep costs down and profits up. But it is a short-term solution for profits, even though the moves offshore may be perma-nent. Innovation cannot be commoditized, for innovation leads to dif-ferentiation because innovative products offer unique value benefits. A process of innovation is a fountain of youth, a source of a profit stream that cannot be quenched from competitive replication. Each innovative solution yields its own differentiated market and unique source of revenues.

Innovation—The New Mandate

Not only are firms returning to innovation as a central source for growth and sustained viability in the competitive marketplace, they also recognize that the greatest growth potential comes from a skill they already possess—growth from within, which is organic growth. An alternative for growing revenues is acquisition. Intelligent acqui-sition is without doubt a valid and important growth strategy. But there are two pitfalls of acquisitions. One pitfall is that it directs the firm's energy and focus outside of the existing firm boundaries, away from existing knowledge, skills, customer insights and loyalties, and brand identity. With attention directed outside the firm, growth opportunities that are in-hand may be unseen or ignored due to man-agement time constraints and corporate budget allocations.

A second pitfall, similar but not identical to the first, is that the company underestimates its own potential for innovation, and it may be tempted to delegate innovation to outside firms. Although outside viewpoints add valuable fresh insights, it is those inside the firm who best know their own customers, who best know their own brand identity, who best understand their own core competencies. New products are not only expressions of a brand or corporate identity, they can also alter identity, for better or for worse. Volkswagen's redesigned Beetle not only expressed the company's history, it modernized its whole brand image, reinvigorating Volkswagen's connection with contemporary culture.

Organic growth—stemming from innovation, knowledge, expertise, and skills already owned by the firm—utilizes rather than ignores the company's latent potential (not growth through acquisitions, nor that ephemeral growth seen only on the balance sheet). Organic growth is growth through innovation and new customers and markets.

But many innovative ideas never see the light of day because commodity-oriented companies are not structured to identify and foster an atmosphere that supports innovation. The intense time-to-market pressures challenge a firm's ability to thoroughly research the product opportunity, and a quality product that is precisely manufactured may fail because it never was a valid concept from the customers' viewpoint. To avoid product failure, many companies follow a rigorous process for intermediary steps of product design. A popular and prototypical one is the StageGate process of Robert G. Cooper.[3] This process creates the structure for timely process to market, with a checklist along the way to make sure the process meets the target schedule and budget. This type of process keeps companies precise. If the right decisions and valid insights are not made in the earlier stages, however, the later stages will not correct a poorly conceived product opportunity. The process will get you to production,

3   Cooper, R. G. *Winning at New Products: Accelerating the Process from Idea to Launch*. Perseus Publishing, Cambridge, 2001.

but you might be producing a product that misses the mark in the marketplace. Unfortunately, mistaking precision and quality manufacture for true product value, which is based on an accurate assessment of one's customers, is sadly common and costly. Unless the product is designed to meet the customer's experiential expectations, the well-made product will fail in the marketplace. We do not argue against a precision-oriented product development process or a well-manufactured product. On the contrary, we believe both are critical for product success. But the best and the average companies today follow those processes. To stand out and deliver value takes more; it takes a process of innovation.

Companies need to develop a culture and mind-set for innovation and organic growth. New companies, such as BodyMedia, are created with this attitude. People are there because they believe in what they are trying to do. They thrive on the challenge. They work in an integrated fashion without turf ownership and friction. Larger companies need to find ways to change the course. They must take their best creative and energetic people and provide an environment that gives them the freedom to innovate. Their success provides the velocity to pull the others along.

Although company culture and mind-set are an important foundation for successful innovation, the challenge is to develop a method to identify and develop a truly innovative product. Although some inventions and innovations have been serendipitous, innovation is generally the result of disciplined activity. Several aspects of innovation and organic growth must come together in a unified strategy in the development and marketing of new products and services. These include an approach to researching the needs, wants, and desires of the target market; an understanding of who the customer is and how the product impacts the end user and indirect users; and an understanding of societal trends. This also includes a rich and unified base of people within a company from the management to the product development team, a corporate culture that encourages and supports innovation, and a complete approach to managing and protecting intellectual property. Finally, a comprehensive process must unify each of these themes in an effective and efficient approach to innovation. These components together represent the product development process of today's most innovative companies.

The Global Dimension of Innovation

In terms of product and service development, three major changes are affecting the world we live in. The first is the balance of global production and consumption; the second is the way products and services are conceived, developed, and delivered; and the third is the perception and expectation of consumers around the world.

As China and India and other less-developed but highly populated regions gain new buying power, the center of gravity of world consumption is shifting from the United States to these larger populaces. Not only are these economies increasingly voracious in terms of consumption quantity, but consumer perceptions and expectations are rising at the same time, as the new wealth allows them to also pursue life, liberty, and happiness.

At the same time, these other countries are gaining new production skills beyond just the ability to manufacture. The United States is certainly still a significant global market for and source of innovation. At the same time, the EU is still evolving as an entity, and new alliances are forming to help countries and companies compete more effectively and open the borders for the development of interconnected markets. Russia is still a question mark but has tremendous potential given its natural resources and population, and the rest of the former Soviet bloc nations are emerging in the global economy as well. Emerging markets in China, India, and several countries in Africa are new growth areas for production and consumption of products and services.

China is now making a major change that will affect all the companies in that country and also worldwide competition. China realizes that to become a serious player in the World Trade Organization, it must be more than the world's leading supply manufacturer. China is not only turning out 300,000 engineers annually, but the country is putting major investment into industrial design. By the year 2010, China will have 500 schools of industrial design. China will become a major source of business, engineering, and design for its own emerging consumer market and will compete in global markets as well. It is already beginning to take over development of new products from former powerhouse engineering countries, such as Germany and the United States. China will follow in the same development path that first occurred in Japan, then in Taiwan and Korea. You might not drive a Hyundai today, but in fewer than 10 years, you will be tempted to buy a car from China from a company that you do not yet even know the name of. Haier has already become a competitor in the United States in refrigerators and TV monitors.

Just a decade ago, China did not have any business schools. Chinese engineering was based on copies of the Russian approach to mechanical and electrical design. Its design schools were either craft schools or based on Russian and East German models of design education and practice. We are witnessing one the fastest movements to modernize in history by the world's largest country. Remember one thing: The Chinese have been here before. Two thousand years ago, China was way ahead of Europe and light years ahead of the Americas. You might not know much about its heritage, but China invented the compass, paper, printing, and gunpowder. This is a country that was "built to last," and it won't have any problems going from "good to great" again.

If China is attempting to become a global competitor based on innovation, and India is close behind, there is no turning back for other countries. Finland is investing huge resources in design and innovation in a program aptly named Finnovation. Building on the early success of Nokia, Finland wants to become a knowledge- and innovation-based country. Even Poland is trying to redesign its brand. It is seeking to rid itself of its image as a land of labor and strife, and is working to bring a fresh look to improve tourism. From countries to companies around the world today, the key is finding a brand strategy that serves as a center for sustained innovation and implementing a method to achieve that strategy—to innovate. The strategy must serve as guide for using methods that promote organic growth and serve evolving needs of consumers as the social, economic, and technological (SET) factors continue to change and produce opportunities for new products and services.

Not only is there a shift in global production capabilities, but the new ease of delivery of product and information is hastening the demise of economic borders. Products and services can now be developed anywhere by anyone and shipped everywhere. Soon, GM will likely sell more Buicks in China than in the United States. Haier has set up a manufacturing and distribution center in South Carolina and is competing in many white goods categories. Samsung recently became a global competitor in design and innovation after decades of being the low-cost option, and its major competitor is Nokia in Finland, not just Motorola.

The media channels that bring information and entertainment into our homes are becoming increasingly global; markets are forming around interests and themes more than geographic location. As fantasy is beamed around the world, everyone is forming his or her own visions of the ideal fashion, car, home interior, and lifestyle experiences. Harry Potter and Michael Jordan transcend geographic limitations. There is an air-conditioned Starbucks in the Forbidden City in Beijing, and there is an Eiffel Tower in both Paris and Las Vegas.

The interplay between the innovative, empowered individual and the forces of global commerce have never been more important. The emerging economies are not threats but sources of endless opportunities. What they all point to is two directions for business strategy. Companies can either choose to be the cheapest, or they can choose to be innovative. This book talks about the latter, because in every market, only one company can be the cheapest, and the competition to be the low-cost provider is fierce. Unlike the lose-lose economics between low-cost competitors, innovation is a win-win that lessens competition among companies by differentiating products, allows producers to increase their prices, and delights customers by providing greater value to them. As companies determine their core values and capabilities, they establish unique brand identities that connect company to consumer. Competing up the price ladder enriches people and companies. It is well demonstrated that people will pay for products they value. As the SET factors continue to shift, the companies that can most effectively read market trends will win.

Surfing the Waves of Innovation

The marketplace emphasis on innovation is not going to go away. It is here to stay, and the rules are not as obvious as in the era of mass consumption and predictable markets. This is very much a hands-on, learn-by-doing world. The people who are having success in this new environment are working hard but having fun. They see the current world as an opportunity, not as an insurmountable challenge. They are surfing the biggest waves with a healthy respect for the forces under the surfboard, but they have overcome the fear of failure and have become the new breed of innovators. These individuals have mastered the process of pragmatic innovation.

3

THE ART AND SCIENCE
OF BUSINESS

Despite the pervasive view that innovation depends on serendipitous inspirations from creative individuals, today's innovative companies rely on disciplined research and procedures to achieve innovation. These procedures for creativity are fundamentally different from what we typically think of as "procedures," but they are procedures nonetheless, and they can be learned, used, and adopted by anyone— anyone, at least, who is willing to intelligently take the uncertainty head on to risk and endure failure in the disciplined quest for a brilliant idea.

Villeneuve d'Ascq, France. Isabelle, a new owner of a pair of Adidas 1s, would not surface as an obvious candidate for this shoe according to demographic studies. She does run for exercise, but she thinks of herself not as a runner but as a mom, a tennis player, and an employee of local canner Bonduelle. She is healthy and active and has won and placed in multiple local tennis tournaments, but she has never participated in any competitive running event.

Isabelle blends into demographic groups; she could be used as a representative of the average educated 40-year-old married woman. She lives in a suburb of Lille, the second most densely populated city in France. The narrow and windy streets feel like walled corridors, passageways lined by a continuum of homes and storefronts that are partially clogged by cars parked half on the street and half on the sidewalk. Isabelle's house shares a wall with a small grocer, a convenient neighbor given her standard French penchant for fresh produce.

Not only is the location of her residence typical, she herself is quite representative in terms of household income and religious and political views. Unlike the few and the loud who end up portrayed on the American news, she likes America, not just its movies. Her dual household income is also typical, being ample for comfortable living while not allowing for abundance. She, like most, is careful in her expenditures, careful in her product choices.

Where this typical French woman *is* unusual is right there—in her product choices. For years, she drove a Dodge Grand Caravan, a great family vehicle but an unusual choice in France. Now she drives a PT Cruiser, for her two girls are older, and the still-roomy but smaller PT Cruiser fits her family's current needs. Although both of these vehicles arguably make sense as functional purchases, both also distinguish her family from others, which is one of her unstated reasons for choosing them in the first place.

Her real excitement in purchasing these automobiles is that they were cutting-edge products in France. What does not show up in a demographic profile of Isabelle is that she is an early adopter of new products. After all, her home was one of the first in the area to have a DVD player, and before that, she was one of the first few to have a Sony videodisc player. When she bought the Adidas 1s, Isabelle convinced herself that her feet needed them, because in truth they are increasingly sore after her jogs. Her shoes are far more to her than running comfort. She is more excited about these shoes than she would be about similarly superb inserts, because the Adidas 1 running shoes are the first of a new generation of products.

Launching the Adidas 1

Athletic apparel companies intensely compete for each customer. In fact, in some ways, their behavior is much like that of their most intense users, the hard-core runners. Many serious runners are slow to change in terms of their routines, training, diet, and equipment. Once they have found a system that works, they stick with it. It becomes their ritual, their passion. They have bought the same model and brand of shoes for years, and they are upset if that model is ever phased out. Other serious runners always look for an edge, even a micro-edge. They are willing to try any change as long as it promises to offer a fraction of a second.

The same goes for the companies such as Adidas, New Balance, and Nike, companies that make the shoes and clothing worn by these hard-core users. These companies simultaneously act like both types of runner. Each company has its core strengths in terms of technology and loyal following. Change here is not an option. At the same time, each vies for a micro-edge relative to its competitors, and each looks to innovation to steal a fraction of market share. So far, each company has independently worked on similar innovation, so not one of them in recent times has put much distance between its own products and those of the competition. All are racing forward, picking up speed rather than tiring, not exactly sure where they are headed but working to stay ahead.

Now Adidas has a revolutionary product—not a micro-edge improvement, but one that promises a substantial lead in the race. The accomplishments of the Adidas 1 have always been a dream in the footwear industry, a fantasy idea on every shoemaker's wish list, because each individual has not just different-size feet, but different cushioning needs. Adjustable cushioning has been discussed in the industry for years, and the solution from Adidas is far superior even to what most have dreamed about. Even more importantly, it is the first of a new generation of products, the first of a new realm of inquiry and innovation.

The Adidas 1 was developed in secrecy in the German company's U.S. headquarters in Portland, Oregon. The Adidas 1 is an intelligent shoe, with a 20-megahertz computer embedded in the arch and linked to a sensor in the heel cushion. Taking up to 20,000 readings every second, the computer-powered shoe constantly measures the impact on the sole. It re-tensions a tiny screw- and cable-system to optimize the shoe's cushioning not only to the runner's size and stride but also to the runner's current speed and terrain, whether concrete or grass. The shoe adjusts itself every fourth step, and all the shifts occur mid-stride so that the runner doesn't feel them and so that the shoe conserves power, extending battery life. If the terrain is too soft, a motor adjusts the cushion so that it is less springy when the runner steps down. If it is too hard, it allows the cushion to expand.

Stephen Pierpoint heads up the marketing of the Adidas 1 in Germany. He grew up a fanatic of consumerism and was keenly brand-oriented at an early age. He studied business at Sheffield University in his home country of England, concentrating primarily on marketing. He took advantage of the range of courses the university offered to not only expand his business knowledge but also to further his interest in the human side of marketing, because he especially enjoyed the creativity of advertising appeal. Both when growing up and later at the university, much of his interest centered around sports, so his marketing role at Adidas was a realization of a lifelong dream.

As of autumn 2004, Pierpoint was in the midst of planning for the March 2005 product launch of the Adidas 1. There is much to be planned, especially because the impact of this launch supersedes that of the product. It is a launch that affects the essence of the Adidas brand worldwide. Central to every product launch is the identification of target consumers. For the Adidas 1, Pierpoint talks about two broad consumer segments. One segment is simply those who would go out and buy the product. These are the early adopters, serious runners who look for new technologies to give them an edge. Adidas wants to make sure these early adopters are fully satisfied by the experience of using the shoes—so satisfied that they will never go back to any old-generation running shoes. So Adidas is being careful in its distribution, deciding not just which countries in which to launch the 1, but which stores in which countries, and how much inventory should go to each of these stores. The company wants to be sure to put the product in front of the right people first. For everything changes from this point forward.

The other segment is the brand audience, the listeners who will be influenced by the message of the product itself. This landmark product not only gives Adidas the ability to change the perception of its whole brand, but it also forces a change in perception, because this product puts Adidas at the forefront of innovation in the athletic apparel industry. The challenge for many product marketers is to think of ways to make the product as new and exciting as possible. The marketing challenge for Pierpoint is probably harder, because his marketing efforts must live up to the true greatness of this very new product.

To convey the story of this new shoe, one focus is how it will appear at the retailer. It is not a typical shoe, so use of the typical packaging would fail to communicate content differences. Another initiative is to write a user manual for the shoe. To those of us who are not writing that user manual, the task appears straightforward. However, this is the first shoe that comes with an instruction manual, so there is no template to follow. Remember how bad the first computer manuals were? Adidas knows that even the simple task of an instruction manual can have a major impact on the image of the whole company, so the manuals are being crafted as carefully as the shoe was designed. One of the reasons why Adidas launched the publicity more than six months before the product was released was to get the idea out there so that it could work with focus groups that were already aware of the product and could read the opinions in chat rooms and on Web sites. Pierpoint wanted to see the types of words used by consumers, to identify any fears that exist so that his team could properly address them. How consumers reacted to the shoe's announcement gives his marketing team a sort of test market to use so that the real product launch goes smoothly.

Pierpoint is not stopping at launch; the planning continues. Adidas has marketing plans beyond the launch for the Adidas 1 and for other shoes. It is already planning the next level of intelligence, laying out a map of how it intends to strategically evolve the product and its extensions.

The Role of Marketing in the Early Stages of Product Development

In the companies that we have worked with, marketing professionals are often not involved directly with innovation. They are involved prior to innovation by setting strategic directions, and they are involved after products are developed to take the product to market. Adidas likewise sets up small innovation teams composed of engineers and designers. Many of their outcomes do not see the light of day. Whenever they are ready to come to life, however, the innovation team is integrated with a marketing team. The teams typically unite smoothly because of their unified focus on the athlete—how to make a difference to the individual athlete, ways to innovatively reach and meet the athlete, recreational or serious.

However, there are also benefits to including marketers on the original innovation teams, not just after the idea is judged a "go." In fact, many marketers do not even perceive that they have the needed skills for innovation and product development. During their studies for their MBA, marketers receive excellent training in how to solve problems, and they are well equipped to recognize ramifications of various solutions and strategies. In the early stages of product development, however, the issue is not to solve a problem but to define it, to recognize and understand the opportunity. Thinking in terms of the case studies used in business schools, business students are taught to analyze case studies, not to write them. Early product work is more like writing the case than analyzing it, of setting up the opportunity rather than deciding how to meet it, of identifying a problem to solve rather than actually solving it.

An emerging trend in business education is to require students to wrestle with ambiguous situations where the facts and issues are not neatly organized into a case study, to practice the kind of skills needed in the fuzzy front end of product development. But even if there is a person with a marketing MBA who is trained only to solve problems and never to define them, even that marketer already has skills that are useful for early product work—skills that help define the opportunity to explore.

Marketers have been trained to study people, to think about why people purchase products. Marketers have learned how to identify segments of consumers, they have studied quantitative methods that describe large groups of potential and real customers, and they have developed measures of advertising reach, brand recognition, and promotion reaction. Traditional marketers' practice of thinking about people is transferable to the type of research needed to identify and explore product opportunities. They just have to learn to see the problem differently, to be comfortable with uncertainty and missing information. They have to make decisions based more on insight and less on irrefutable fact, because the facts simply are not available at the early stages of innovation.

Another beneficial characteristic of marketers is that they tend to keep close tabs on business needs, even while they are busy in the field of understanding customers. When marketers are involved in the early development process, their constant attention to business perspective aids alignment of product and brand, of product and corporate strategy. Built in to the marketing discipline is an economic perspective, that consumers are economic agents whose purchases balance costs with benefits. Engineers have a keen mind toward what is possible, regardless of need. Industrial designers bring in those strong forces that cause double-takes, such as beauty, and create features that ease implementation and pleasure of use. The cross-functional synthesis of all of these perspectives leads to a workable and exciting solution.

The Ambiguity of Figuring Out Winning Products

Early product development entails numerous choices, and it seems at first glance like these choices could be 100 percent left brain or analytical activity. For instance, the product development team at Adidas had to choose whether to bring out separate men's and women's shoes or to make a unisex shoe. They could have made this decision an analytical activity by surveying potential consumers to see what customers want, just like U.S. presidents have been known to use focus groups to test policy ideas. Similarly, a product development team makes many other decisions, questions that they answer one way or another. In the Adidas 1, the sensors assess the sole's compression, affected by weight, terrain, and runner's speed, but the design team could also have incorporated a pedometer and calorie counter, as Puma AG considered doing back in the late 1980s. Should the Adidas 1 include a pedometer? In other words, would sales be higher if the model had a pedometer, or lower, or would it even matter? Until this is tested, the answer is unknown. Although the current shoe is not equipped with a link to a desktop or laptop, the in-shoe computer could conceivably have an outlet to download information into a laptop. What would happen to sales? Or the shoe could have a wireless transmitter to send data to a handheld PDA. Would sales be higher? Similarly, the design team has chosen to show off the circuitry via a clear plastic panel, but that, too, was a factor that could have been optimized. How are costs affected by the clear panel? Will sales be higher? Adidas's first smart shoe did not need to be designed for running—it could have targeted soccer, a sport Adidas has long dominated and a core area of its expertise. The possibilities are seemingly endless. Each decision can be tested in an experiment, like a test market. But not all decisions can be tested; there are just too many.

Without market tests that would show which integrated features are the best combination for the marketplace, it is not clear what exact product the company should develop to achieve the greatest improvement to the lives of customers and to the company's bottom line. The answers to the choices (exact product specifications) are ambiguous rather than clear. Answers are ambiguous because information is lacking, but decisions still must be made. Decisions here are not safe, and ramifications of decisions are unpredictable.

A Sound Basis for Vision (Yes, You Can Go with Your Instinct)

Ambiguity is common, especially in innovation, and it is the uncommon individual who has the vision to make good decisions when dealing with ambiguity. These individuals must be willing to take a stand in spite of lack of hard evidence, and they personally shoulder the risks of their choices. These are managers like Dee Kapur, Chuck Jones, Edith Harmon, and the others mentioned in other chapters in this book. Rather than relying solely on results of experiments, they arm themselves with vision. Rather than waiting for overwhelming evidence of a correct path before moving forward, they use existing knowledge, experience, and resources.

By necessity or by training, innovators are comfortable with uncertainty. But not all of us are. Think about yourself. How comfortable are you making decisions without hard evidence? Would you defend human judgment as scientifically valid? Suppose, for example, that you and a friend cannot remember who paid for lunch last time, so you decide to flip a coin to see who pays today. You pull a U.S. quarter from your pocket, and you notice that it is one of the new quarters, each of which features a different state; this one is from Texas. If you are typical, you would not think twice about using that coin to decide who pays for lunch, even though you have never flipped any of the new Texas quarters before. If someone asked you whether you knew for certain that the coin was "fair," you would have to agree that you do not know the exact probabilities, that one outcome may be slightly more likely than the other. Should that coin be used without further investigation? Should you first test it, maybe flipping it 1,000 times to see whether you get around 500 "heads"?

Most of us would use the coin without ever thinking about testing it. Put another way, we would simply assume that coin has equal chances of heads and tails. Would you be able to justify such an assumption? If you strictly apply the teaching of the typical required college statistics class, you would argue that you have no idea of the probability of a heads on a Texas quarter until you see some evidence. Yet, even while reading this, you probably still think it is close to being fair. Why? Is it not equally plausible that heads will show 9 times out of 10? The quarter could be more heavily weighted on the side that shows the state—everyone know that Texas is a really big state!

Science does support your gut here—that you can reasonably believe the coin is "fair" even though you have never tested it. How so? A relatively new statistical system, Bayesian statistics, supports the use of past information (such as experience) to help current decisions. You have probably flipped many coins over your lifetime, even though you have never flipped a Texas quarter. Because coins in your lifetime have been fair, or close enough to fair, your natural reaction with the new coin is to believe it also is fair, at least until proven otherwise. The formal, simple framework of your college statistics class would say you know nothing about the Texas coin until testing it. The Bayesian statistics framework would say that your wealth of experience with coin flipping is exactly what you should believe about this coin until it proves to be any different. The Bayesian statistics framework has revolutionized modern research methods. It is used as the basis for Internet search engines, e-mail spam filters, artificial intelligence systems, pharmaceutical tests, and much more.

Certainly, the Bayesian framework does not give you license to unbridled opinion and postulating. It does not toss out scientific rigor. You need the rigor of the Bayesian, the recognition of valid data, the discipline to throw away the irrelevant, the willingness to dive into the uncertain, and the care not to become overconfident. But it also tells us that educated insight has merit, just like statistical validation.

This world is that of the innovator—the simple acceptance of uncertainty, a willingness to make decisions in spite of a lack of information that reveals the "right" decision. The innovators' familiarity with ambiguity has shaped their mind-set, has led them to see ways to improve their world that may be missed by others.

A Process for Pragmatic Innovation

The natural question, then, is how to innovate. As Peter Drucker and others have written before, innovation is not serendipity but the outcome of disciplined activity. What is the nature of that disciplined activity? What kinds of procedures can be adopted that can and will yield good ideas when so many decisions must be made—too many to answer via experimentation?

In his book *The Sciences of the Artificial*,[1] economics Nobel Laureate Herb Simon describes the science of design. He recognizes that "exact solutions to the larger optimization problems of the real

1 Simon, H. A. *The Science of the Artificial*. The MIT Press, Cambridge, MA, 1969.

world are simply not within reach or sight. In the face of this complexity the real-world business firm turns to procedures that find good enough answers to questions whose best answers are unknowable." Simon invented the word *satisficing* to describe this situation, in which a person "accepts 'good enough' alternatives not because he prefers less to more but because he has no choice." Product innovation is not about optimizing but satisficing.

The procedures he suggests are to set goals and make decisions relative to those goals. Rather than the impossible task of optimization, in which one would ask, "Of all possible worlds, which is the best?," the question in innovation is, "Does this alternative satisfy all the design criteria in a preferred way?" A challenge for satisficing in innovation, then, is to define the criteria for success.

Akin to the philosophy of Herb Simon, we will articulate a sequence of steps and procedures for the earliest stages of innovation that the best innovators seem to follow. This early part of the product development process is often called the "fuzzy front end" because it is counter to the precise facts known about the product in the later stages, where the product is detailed for production. In brief, the early tasks set up the criteria, not from irrefutable fact but from insights based on user observation, and the later tasks create product alternatives that meet those criteria. This process is equally useful in designing products as well as services. We highlight these procedures here, we discuss many aspects of them throughout this book, and we illustrate the details of this sequence of steps in the process in Chapter 9, "A Process for Product Innovation."

Identify an Area of Strategic Importance

First, pick a general area of strategic importance to the company or target market. This could be a key market for your company, such as baby boomer males who run aggressively. This general area narrows down the scope of research and development, making it feasible rather than impossible. Of course, it also helps ensure that the work being performed is consistent with the company's goals.

Research People

Research the people and the social, economic, and technological factors (also called the SET factors) related to that area. We discuss SET trends in Chapter 4, "Identifying Today's Trends for Tomorrow's Innovations." As for the people, innovators need to research real people, to get to know actual individuals of importance to their strategic domain. We emphasize "real" people in order to steer research away from aggregate statistics that describe groups of people. We hold no ill will toward statistics, but statistics generally provide answers to questions that have been important year after year. To a great extent, then, statistics answer old questions, and innovation is all about the present and the future. Another problem with statistics is that they provide simplified, summarized, arms-length knowledge of people. Without direct interaction with real people, innovators do not truly know these key individuals; they just know a limited set of facts about "typical" people in a target set.

Coincidentally, Simon was also a psychologist. He spoke of protocol analysis where, rather than studying the masses, one studies only a few people in depth to understand their process and approach to solving a problem. Extensive surveys provide a rich quantity of information, but the survey is only as good as the questions asked and the validity of the people as a cohort of the market who answer them. At the fuzzy front end, the innovator doesn't yet know what to ask and therefore cannot refine a questionnaire to identify who the masses are.

Innovation is all about people, not products. It is about the team inside the company that has the role of innovating as well as the people outside the company who interact with or are impacted by the innovation. Because people are central to innovation, we have filled our book with people. We began in Chapter 1, "The New Breed of Innovator," with biographical sketches of a handful of innovators. Chapter 6, "The Powers of Stakeholders—People Fueling Innovation," discusses analysis of product "stakeholders." Also every chapter begins with a scenario of a prototypical individual using a product.

The rest of the activities in innovation are best learned by doing them. As such, in Chapter 9 we illustrate the steps described next in the context of an actual project. If you want to read more, we also have described these steps in detail in *Creating Breakthrough Products: Innovation from Product Planning to Program Approval.*[2]

Define the Opportunity

The dynamics of trends are constantly providing new opportunities in the marketplace, and the research and knowledge of key stakeholders will reveal multiple opportunities within the specified strategy area. Using an analogy, an opportunity is to a product as a problem is to a solution. The opportunity is a positive way to define a current state, and a product is the goal of the desired state. Here, the objective is not to think of products but of what products will achieve for people—what are the needs, wants, and desires of the opportunity. What do the people you researched value that is not currently provided?

Define Design Criteria

Based on that research, what characteristics does a product need to have (not what should a product look like) to fulfill the desired state of the opportunity? These characteristics are the design criteria.

2 Cagan, J. and C. M. Vogel. *Creating Breakthrough Products: Innovation from Product Planning to Program Approval.* Financial Times Prentice Hall, Upper Saddle River, NJ, 2002.

Achieve the Criteria

Develop numerous product ideas that can potentially meet the criteria, and prototype the most promising ideas that do meet the criteria. Obtain feedback from target users about the prototypes, and iteratively redesign until the product design seems to be the best you can make it, or at least within the criteria you defined.

Go/No-Go Decision

The product now is specified well enough to make a go/no-go decision. At this point, if it is judged worthy to pursue, the product enters a new phase, into preparation for production and product launch. For some companies, this is the point at which the innovation team leaves this product and starts afresh on others. We like the approach of Adidas, which at this point integrates the innovation team with a marketing team so that expertise and momentum are not lost in transfer. One improvement to Adidas's already great innovation structure would be to have had marketers on the innovation teams along with designers and engineers.

The Ground Rules: Understanding the Innovator's View of Procedures

These steps for satisficing-based product development are fundamentally different from what we typically think of as "procedures." Even so, they are methods, and therefore they can be learned, adopted, and used by anyone. But because of how much they differ from other procedures with which most people are familiar, we here step back from the methods and discuss how they are to be used and what to expect from them. In particular, we cover four aspects of methods for innovation: 1) the methods require the user to work and

think, 2) the methods cannot mass-produce ideas, 3) company investment should be in the process rather than the outcomes, and 4) the
methods require not just intelligence but internal motivation. We
contrast these four points with the "For Dummies" series of books so
that you will understand the different nature of the decision philosophy and mentality of innovators.

Point 1: Thinking Required

Many of us prefer to improve ourselves and our world without risk,
without uncertainty. We like step-by-step guaranteed procedures,
such as those of the "_____ for Dummies" books. Fill in the blank
any way you want—someone has written it. You can buy *Low-Carb
Dieting for Dummies, Catholicism for Dummies, Guitar for
Dummies, Japanese for Dummies, NASCAR for Dummies*, and even
Sex for Dummies. When we recently searched its Web site, Barnes &
Noble listed 2,519 entries that are "for dummies." These titles offer
methods that eliminate uncertainty, procedures that are no-brainer
methods for guaranteed success, improvement without risk.

Of course, the "For Dummies" type of procedure is widely
embraced. Such procedures for risk-free improvement have yielded
large profits and have benefited society for countless years. Consider
technology available to farmers over centuries. An ox-drawn plow was
certain to yield gains relative to a human-powered hoe. Then mech-
anized solutions (such as tractors) offered still greater profits; farmers
could cultivate more land per hour and thus obtain greater revenues
for the same hour of labor. There is no uncertainty—a farm with
mechanical equipment will be able to produce a larger harvest, per
labor hour, than a farmer using Amish-approved techniques. A more
modern example comes from a mathematical research field called
"operations research," the science of optimal business decisions.
Operations researchers provide schedules for airlines and baseball
seasons, figure out the best locations for product warehouses, and

devise inventory management policies so that retailers do not waste precious capital on items that sit on shelves for most of the year. These scheduling formulas, inventory management solutions, and other operations research techniques offer risk-free improvements, like tractors for farmers. The improvements can be worth vast sums to the company. For instance, John Deere recently saved $1 billion through the supply-chain tinkering of SmartOps, an operations research consulting firm.

With a "For Dummies" checklist, it is the process that does the work. The person implementing the process does not matter, does not need to think—hence the series title. But with the methods for innovation, the user of the methods is critical, for the methods aid but do not replace the innovator. They enable the innovator. They are a tool, like a hammer for a carpenter, and like computer-aided design (CAD) in the hands of an architect. The Freedom Tower in New York has been designed using the latest development in CAD tools, a 3D drawing and modeling program called Revit. Similar programs have long been used by engineers and designers in the design of motorcycles, airplanes, and other consumer products. The tool tremendously leverages the ability of the architect, but the architect still must do the work. Methods of innovation are tools that leverage the skills of the user, tools that take that person's productivity beyond what it would be otherwise.

Consider the work of Frank Gehry, the famous architect who designed, among other masterpieces, the Guggenheim Museum in Bilbao, Spain. Gehry's buildings are large-scale livable art forms that flow and curve in ways only imaginably drawn on paper or molded in clay. Yet these organic shapes that meet and multiply at many levels of complexity form the basis for Gehry's buildings. There is no repetition or standardization; no two forms or parts of forms on his buildings are the same. One can imagine what a nightmare to the traditional construction contractor must be the daunting task of constructing one of these buildings. Yet they are envisioned, designed, and then successfully built. The only way that this can happen is with the tool of CAD/CAM. The CAD system allows Gehry to represent and communicate his imagination. The CAM (computer-aided manufacturing) system allows each piece of material on the outside of the building to be individually manufactured and labeled for assembly. The CAD/CAM system, in this case one called CATIA, is just a tool, but in the hands of his engineers, it is a sophisticated enabler that allows Gehry's innovation to become a commercial and structural success.

Point 2: Innovation Yields Differentiation

A second aspect of the methods is that they are not for mass production. Thinking again of the CAD example, a tour through Houston suburbs shows that houses can be mass-produced, through replication and permutation of components. But innovation is sorely lacking. The Houston suburb is no Bilbao.

It isn't the fact that these methods are difficult to understand that prevents mass production. Even complex mathematical equations can be reduced to a "For Dummies" framework; they can be simplified to the point-and-click of software, and any competitor in any country can then adopt that method. Methods for innovation have a nice advantage over those that can be mass-produced, because they require smart people. They are not "For Dummies." If you are that smart person, your job stays with you. Your job cannot be coded into software that ships throughout the world to legions of replacements for you. If your company has a process for innovation, a greenhouse for organic growth, your innovations become competitive advantages, not commodities that spread quickly to imitators worldwide.

Point 3: Don't Stop at Success

A third aspect of the methods is that they should be part of a larger process, an incubator to grow ongoing innovations. Innovation is risky; the failure rate is high. Consider for a moment an industry that makes a business of risk: casinos. The big money of the speculative world comes from a system of speculations, not a single gamble. The "house" may lose any gamble—it never knows which ones will pay off and which will not. But the odds are in its favor, so repetition yields its lucre. Although the statistics on new product success rates reveal low winning probabilities, the lesson is the same—that repetition is important. With innovation, any particular project may fail dismally. It is repetition of the process that yields the payoff. You can, however, slant the odds in your favor; you can beat the house odds in the introduction of new products if you have the right tools and methods and diligently follow them. Certainly don't stop at success—keep the greenhouse intact in order to keep growing new ideas.

Many innovative companies do put mechanisms in place to constantly feed the innovation cycle. Lubrizol, a company that develops "fluid technologies for a better world" that we discuss later in this book, has a process by which every year two new technologies are developed into product possibilities. In the first chapter, Chuck Jones talked about a constant stream of product ideas that are in the pipeline at Whirlpool. Other companies support advanced R&D to develop new areas of growth. New Balance, also discussed in this book, has a strong advanced product group that constantly seeks not only new product opportunities, but also new approaches to determining those opportunities. Still other companies create divisions to support new growth. For example, Respironics, a maker of sleep apnea and support products, formed a division for "sleep onset" to recognize the emerging technologies and growing demand for products to help people sleep and sleep better.

Point 4: Motivation Needed

Finally, the methods for innovation are not a step-by-step guarantee for success, unlike the promise of the "For Dummies" series. In the hands of an unmotivated employee, the methods yield no benefit. As an illustration, compare Kate and Susan. Kate has the entrepreneur-ial spirit, that inward drive to maximize the possibilities around her. In college, she took pride in her work (for most classes, at least). For instance, for her case study analyses in marketing class, she read more on the company than what was presented in the preprinted case study. She put herself into the role of the decision maker, researched competitor companies and their strategies, and took the time to think seriously about the actual and potential customers of each company.

Susan also was diligent and hard-working in school, but her goal was mainly to get an A on each project. In her marketing class, she made sure to discuss each of marketing's "four Ps" (price, product, place of distribution, and promotion). Her motivation was external—to fulfill the letter of the law, to get the letter grade. For Susan, the instructions did the work for her; she basically filled in the blanks, and she got her A.

Both Kate and Susan have found jobs in which they are success-ful, but only Kate would be successful with the methods for innova-tion. Susan's approach to work is to fill in the blanks of a "For Dummies" process; Kate's approach is to use the process to gain deep-er insights. The world of innovation is all about deeper insights. There is no forward and upward movement when the blanks are just filled in.

The innovators' methods that we describe are best practices, used by the successful innovating companies. They are like CAD for the architect, a framework and set of tools to improve innovation. They are insufficient by themselves for successful innovation, because they require the motivation like that of entrepreneurs, like that of Kate. The methods just become more paperwork for the Susans of the world, but the same methods allow the Kates to be ingenious, to make an impact, and to stand out from the fray. Overall, these meth-ods serve as the early stages of product research, a repeatable process to find and develop successful innovative products.

4

IDENTIFYING TODAY'S TRENDS FOR TOMORROW'S INNOVATIONS

In light of the opportunities that are already here in the present, there is no reason to long for unavailable crystal ball forecasts of future prospects. The earliest work of innovation is to research existing trends and to understand them in the context of customers, because it is market dynamics that provide new opportunities that will be fulfilled by tomorrow's successful products.

New York, NY. Fredrick Marano put down *Newsweek*. The article on iPod's explosive sales growth had caught his eye because he very much enjoyed his iPod. For Fred, most products were extras—good appendages, but appendages nonetheless. The iPod was different, more central. Fred remembered his first Walkman. Big, bulky, heavy (at least in comparison to nowadays). A cassette tape player that jammed and jumped as he exercised. All the hassles of having to tape LP music.

It was clear to Fred why the iPod fared so well: It was the right product at the right time. The iPod is great. Stylish and easy to use. Any music he had or wanted to buy, he could download. He had just started using iTunes, a service to download individual songs for 99 cents. The last time he purchased an individual song was back in the days of vinyl in the 1980s when he used to go to CBGBs on the Lower East Side! It took Fred awhile to feel comfortable paying for something he could not hold. He can download a song, but it exists only on his iPod or computer. He cannot touch it. But he also is not stuck with a CD full of songs he does not want to listen to anyhow.

Most of the music Fred listens to on his iPod, he copied over from his collection of CDs. Much like he used to do with his cassettes, he chuckled to himself. Well, they had the idea right, but not the medium. Now all he has to do is pop in a CD, pick a track, and click a button. The rest is magic. As far as he could figure out, it really was magic. But it worked and worked well; so, like everything else today, he will go with the flow as long as he doesn't have to think about it.

Fred's teenage daughter, Liz, was always getting new music on her MP3. She kept telling Fred to go on Kazaa to get his music. She got most of her music that way. CDs are so overpriced, and who needs them cluttering up her room?

Liz and her friends believed it was their right. No bureaucratic corporate giant had the right to charge 20 bucks for a CD. Most mega bands had too much money already, and most independent groups who did not play the game made no money. It was her right to listen to what she wanted whether or not big business decided to mass-produce it.

Fred did not believe in piracy for himself, but he did not make a big deal of it to Liz. She was one of a million kids doing this. But Fred did like the idea of being able to change his music selection in minutes, and to store hundreds of songs on his tiny player.

Ah, yes, the smallness of current players provides an incredible benefit. Besides being cool-looking and so intuitive, the iPod is truly small. How does it store 10,000 songs? 10,000 songs would fill 750 CDs, which would take up a bookcase in his study! Instead, he can go running with it clipped to his belt, and the quality of sound is as good as it gets.

The iPod is not the only small player, for it is the MP3 technology that allows it to be small. One of Fred's friends at work has had an MP3 player for years now. But, then, that guy always had to have new gadgets first, even if he stayed up all night figuring them out. Fred always could tell what was coming down the road by talking with his friend, but he also waited until he knew he would not have hassles.

Lead Users and New Technology

MP3 technology was developed in the mid-1980s in Germany. All digital music, be it on CD or in MP3 format, is stored as 1s and 0s, or bits. A typical song is 32 megabytes (MB) of data, or 256,000,000 bits. A CD can store close to 800 MB, meaning 74 minutes in practice, or essentially an album. MP3 is a format that compresses the data by removing information that either the human ear cannot hear or that is much quieter than other sounds, making them hard to hear. This allows storage of almost the same quality music in one-tenth the number of bits. So a CD could now store 10 albums! The issue for portability is certainly size. MP3 players either work through "flash," where songs are stored on a stationary medium, or through small hard drives, as with the iPod. Either way, there is limited storage space that, if each bit had to be stored, would make it impossible to store enough songs to keep the consumer happy in the small space of the player. MP3, and other compressed digital audio formats, such as the one iTunes uses, is a technological breakthrough that was a tipping point in making portable digital music desirable.

For any new technology, there is always a group of innovators who enjoy the cutting edge, the lead users who tolerate usability glitches in order to own the benefits of the new features. The purchases of lead users can serve as early indicators of trends, of changes in opportunities. But it is critical to keep in mind that lead user purchases point to new opportunities rather than to new products that will eventually hit big time; after all, the solutions that lead users tolerate do not necessarily "cross the chasm" into mainstream purchase.

The iPod, for instance, was not new technology. Since the late 1990s, there had been several MP3 players on the market. With a bit of research, innovators had been able to find MP3 players that met their functional needs—reliable MP3 music with a usable interface. For everybody else, the majority of people, it was an abstract technology for kids and nerds. As Geoffrey Moore[1] would say, there was a chasm or gap between the small group of early adopters and the large early majority market who liked new technology as long as it was a complete product. In this case, cultural and economic trends had readied the majority market for a complete product and had provided opportunity for the insightful company.

Apple: Trend Reader

This is where Apple came in. In the computer industry, Apple is known as the innovator. The rest follow. Apple has consistently provided models of where the industry needs to go. Most PC manufacturers have made commodities, computers that are exchangeable parts housed in generic dark gray boxes. No wonder companies such as Gateway struggle, fighting for razor-thin profit margins, for such is the natural way of commodities. For the first time

1   Moore, G. *Crossing the Chasm.* Harper Perennial, New York, 1999.

in the history of computers, saturation at the new millennium brought a slump in sales, and PC manufacturers are hit hard, because thin margins require large sales volumes. Apple, on the other hand, understands that this is the experience economy, and it has maintained price premiums by focusing on the user experience. Apple has even moved its product beyond the experience economy to appeal to the nascent fantasy economy, which we describe in the next chapter. The line of iMacs are examples of high-styled products that rely on more than just the latest technology. Apple is a trend reader.

Of course, not all of Apple's products have been perfect. Trend reading does not offer the imaginary promise of a look into a crystal ball. Apple went wrong by maintaining a proprietary operating system, insisting on delivering a complete hardware and software product. Because it kept competitors out, fewer Macs were available to the market. Fewer Macs meant fewer programs being written for them. Then, in the mid-1990s, as the personal computer market flourished, Apple sought to join the other manufacturers in their Wal-Mart strategy—high volume and low costs. Apple fired innovator Steve Jobs and hired businessman John Scully. Scully focused on cutting costs and strayed from the company's innovation mantra. The resulting lackluster products and poor quality almost sent Apple into bankruptcy. The return of Steve Jobs brought Apple back on the path to innovation, and Apple flourishes again after retaking the smaller but premium market. In spite of these problems, Apple has consistently brought out insightful products that other companies end up imitating. Apple is an ideas leader, consistently better at anticipating trends because it reads the trends, and its ideas not only tap pools of lead users but cross the chasm to the mainstream.

Focusing back on MP3s, the technology existed, and lead users had it, but no product had grabbed the attention of the rest of the market. Companies that are adept at developing new products recognize such situations and have learned to use design as a means to translate barely useable technology into useful, useable, and desirable products. For instance, Palm Computing built the wildly successful PDA out of the ashes of Apple's Newton, Sharp's Wizard, Microsoft's

WinPad, and others. Technology is part of the equation, but equally important is the user interaction, ergonomics, and lifestyle features. Palm's first PDA had a form factor far smaller than its predecessors and was truly portable and therefore usable. Apple's computers, for example, have technical capability, are easy to use, and also look great. They set the standard rather than follow. They are the first products in the computer industry that look so good that they become the focus of a room rather than the blemish.

The same is true for the iPod. The iPod itself defines the contemporary aesthetic for portability with its simple lines and white plastic shell and its intuitive and easy-to-navigate interface through its click wheel. At 6 ounces, it is light and fits in your pocket. But Apple went further. As if the iPod weren't small enough, sleek enough, or beautiful enough, Apple introduced the iPod mini, which weighs less than 4 ounces, is significantly smaller, and comes in a variety of anodized aluminum finishes, and then Apple introduced the even smaller iPod shuffle.

All the uncertainty feared by the early majority is missing from this product. It is hip and cool, it is easy to use, it is affordable, and it is produced from a company that people trust. Apple invested in a great advertising campaign that communicates the positive experience in making the product a part of the individual by having the silhouette of an X- or Y-gen dancing to tunes with his or her iPod. In sum, it is the product that is taking the compressed digital audio format across the chasm.

So How Does One Read Trends?

Trends provide immense profit opportunities to those who read them and can leverage their power. Niall FitzGerald, of Unilever and Reuters fame, talked about trends being analogous to the ocean waves and companies as surfers, saying, "You can be the best surfer in the world. But if you sit with your surfboard on a flat ocean, you won't go very far."[2] If the ocean had no waves, there would be no surfing. If the world were not dynamic, there would be no new opportunities to propel corporate growth. The companies that recognize the trends can be borne along on their energy.

As a first reaction to the idea of "trend reading," many people assume that the task is to foretell the future. But the real task is to understand the present and the dynamics in the present tense and to use that to anticipate future successes. This approach is called "anticipatory design," and it is used by cutting-edge, consistently innovative companies. In many cases, extrapolation to the future is straightforward after one understands the present. For instance, a well-known trend is the aging of the baby boomer generation. Once recognized in the present tense, some future implications are crystal clear, such as the increasing need for medical devices and health-care products.

As an aid to identifying and understanding trends, we use a framework of three broad areas: social, economic, and technological. The idea is that these three main categories are a dynamic window into what the market has and what it wants. In other words, it helps you see where there are gaps between what products are on the market and where there are opportunities to introduce new products. We call these *product opportunity gaps*.

The social factor looks at a market's cultural, lifestyle, and political aspects. The economic factor focuses on a market's buying power and buying focus. The technological factor summarizes advances in new uses for technology within a niche area. The social, economic, and technological (SET) factors summarize a given, often narrow, market segment or focus. They are dynamic and can be driven by or lagged by any one of the factors. The goal is for any company to constantly read these factors and look for opportunities to create new products. The power behind the factors is that they are constantly changing. The best companies read these factors in the present tense and react to changes as they occur.

2   *The Wall Street Journal*. "On Buy-and-Purge Strategy, Need to Keep Changing." May 24, 2004.

Not all changes can be easily accommodated. Not all present wonderful opportunities that can be leveraged by all. Consider the catastrophe of 9/11, which adversely affected international travel but boosted local travel industries in the United States such as snowmobiling. Or consider Ford and Firestone after the Explorer tire explosions, an adverse trend for them. Ford was one of the prime auto companies to be followed by all the rest of the industry until this tragedy. The system could not react quickly enough to the tire problem, and Ford's position in the market declined. This was only part of the problem. The economy had burst, and Ford had invested many resources in the purchase of companies under former CEO Jac Nassar. But clearly, the bad press and concern for safety in a vehicle that was supposed to be safer than the rest led to mistrust of the company and a decline in Explorer sales. The good news for the Ford system is that the impact was temporary. The system had enough robustness to slowly recover and regain market share.

But even the recognition that not all trends are helpful to all industries does not belie the argument that companies succeed by a keen understanding of their competitive marketplace. Exceptionally innovative companies are helped or hurt by good luck or bad luck, but at the same time, they provide consistent insights that provide a constant stream of revenues during good and bad economic times.

Companies such as Apple that can consistently introduce great products have learned to read those trends and are leaders of industry. Often, the products of tomorrow emerge from trends; at times, they create the trends.

Products Impacting Trends

Thinking back to trends as ocean waves and companies as surfers, an aspect of the analogy is interestingly incomplete. Although surfers enjoy the dynamic thrill of the waves, they do not reorient the waves themselves. Their position is changed by the waves, but their little surfboards do not change the direction of the ocean's temperamental flow. However, products do impact trends at the same time that trends impact products. The iPod as a product and MP3 as a technology are both reacting to and setting trends and expectations. MP3 technology allows consumers far more flexibility and demand in music than ever before. People download only the songs they want. The need for physical product gives way to choice and variety. For those who download complete CDs, there are Web sites from which the CD cover can be printed. But for many, the album cover is no longer needed or desired. The social aspects of sharing move to a new level with international participation in shareware sites.

Even before MP3s were developed, music and entertainment delivery systems were continuing the drive toward miniaturization. Smaller is better, and the inconvenience of needing any physical device is compensated for with the iPod through another Apple trend-setting aesthetic and lifestyle statement. For the early adopters, what is next is MP3 in every product that is a part of their life. Even cars today offer MP3 technology. The logistical problems and inconvenience of downloading music to the car stereo is still a roadblock to cross the chasm. But it will happen, and soon MP3 and downloaded music will be the norm.

The iPod holds more music than most people own and organizes it far better than most people organize their CD collection. The concept of portability has implications for producers of environments where people listen to music. Already BMW includes a connection for iPods within some cutting-edge-performance vehicles; customers can take their entire music collection into their car, play it over 10 speakers, and then take it with them when they leave. Also, high-quality speaker systems with an iPod docking station are available for the home and office, effectively replacing the traditional stereo system.

Never before has a music technology been driven by the consumer instead of the recording industry. Kazaa and Limewire are, today, replacements for the original Napster. Shareware software allows each participant to download music from the hard disks of others on the system and to make their music available to others in the same way. The desire and ability to access any music at any time immediately is an expectation of the Y generation today. It is also an illegal exchange format that, through the power and benefits of the Internet, is difficult at best to track down and stop. The original understanding that an individual can copy for himself or herself purchased music has been pushed to a new dimension. Of course, people used to make copies of their albums for their friends. But one, two, or even the occasional hundred copies were noise in the music industry's sales and profits. Today, in theory, one sale of one CD can be distributed to everyone in the world. All they need is Kazaa and someone to fork over $19.95 for the first copy to put online. Although many who use these shareware programs leave the music on their computer or MP3 player, it can easily be copied onto a CD with any burner, creating a perfect copy of an album for anyone who desires it.

The music industry did not push the technology to new formats; instead, the industry has fought the new platform tooth and nail. Lawsuits and arrests to keep shareware sites off the Internet, or at least people off those sites, show the fear the industry rightly feels. For those isolationists who fear the impact China will have on our economy, the answer is that it is reality; learn to work with China rather than fight it. The same is true here. The Internet and compact digital audio technology have changed the business model for the recording industry. Instead of fighting it, the industry must look to new ways to earn the consumer's business—something it has never had to face. Instead of overpricing CDs, companies must look to provide added features to those who buy their product. They must demonstrate in their product the expected morals that people demand so that honesty of purchasing a product wins out over the piracy of Kazaa.

The impact on all of this for the Y and X generations is the demand for more. What they want. When they want it. Now. And free! The reality of the MP3 concept has reinforced the need and demand for immediate gratification.

For the long term, the implication for the music industry is to revisit what it means to be part of the emerging fantasy economy. The industry will produce more singles more often and fewer albums. It will price them at what consumers believe is a reasonable cost. It will support smaller artists. It will recognize that independent record companies have a legitimate business and place in the industry—that, like the MP3 players, bigger is not better. For the consumer as well, the quality of new music will improve. People will have the ability to preview for free anything they would consider buying. The music companies will have to provide a positive enough experience through quality sound and production to earn the purchase of that song. Trust will drive the relationship between the industry and the consumer.

For the majority of people who will pay for the service of downloading music, the virtual stores to purchase the music will become commodities. Services like iTunes will become the Wal-Mart of music everywhere on the Internet (and Wal-Mart now has a music download service). Opportunities will emerge for high-value services that provide more than just access to the music. These services will offer suggestions for music that meet an individual's tastes and will learn what a person likes and dislikes. They will offer virtual and possibly physical social experiences that encourage use of their service. They will provide access to quality entertainment-delivery systems far beyond the transfer of songs to MP3 players.

On a broader scale, the impact of compressed digital audio goes beyond music and entertainment. Businesses need to have accelerated product introductions with more rapid time-to-market development processes. Mass customization will become the norm, where consumers will choose what features they want in a product and what color and style it will be. Nokia was an early proponent of mass customization in what is called "postponement." Consumers not only choose the style phone they want, they can also choose from 50 or more faceplates that allow them to express who they are. Nokia can design and manufacture those faceplates at the last minute to have the most up-to-date style, "postponing" the design of that part. In the future, people will create their own expression in almost every major product they purchase.

Personalization, immediate gratification, and immediate accessibility of the digital music realm spills out into the rest of life; it is part of the future of product development. Companies are constantly developing or seeking out technology to help them produce more, faster, cheaper, and smaller with higher differentiation. This is a global trend. There are others.

In Reading Trends, It Is All About People

There are a host of trends to consider at the outset of product development, forcing those considering trends to identify which are the most relevant to the task at hand. One way to help do so is to frame

the trends in the context of the product users or other product stakeholders. For the rest of this chapter, we use Herman Miller's Mirra
chair as an example of how trends can be identified and presented in
the context of a person, a representative of a key customer type, Tom.

Tom had become an expert on chairs. Not because he was interested in fashion trends in the furniture industry, but simply because,
at the age of 50, he was suffering from severe back problems. Like
many aging baby boomers, Tom was facing an illness that had evolved
over the past decade. The doctor called it a life-limiting illness, but
Tom had no time for limitations.

After the proper diagnosis was made, that his back problem was a
form of arthritis, the challenge was how to thrive in spite of a disabili-
ty that affects not only every moment of your waking life but also your
sleep. Office seating, more accurately called task seating, is a major
challenge to back comfort. Tom started looking into the different types
of chairs available to him at work and found that none of them were
comfortable, especially over time. He had been able to sample a few,
but each time, he ended up using the money-back guarantee. His car
seat was better than most seats he sat in at home or at work, and he
could not figure out why no one could make a chair as comfortable as
his car seat. His wife stumbled on a catalog at a friend's house, the
friend with all the "designer" furniture. Not that her friend's furniture
was any more comfortable than his own; it was a style thing. Even so,
he browsed the catalog, Design Within Reach (DWR), finding chairs
that never appeared in the local Office Depot inventory. One in particular, called the Aeron chair, interested him because he had seen
that chair become popular in high-flying dot-coms. What caught his
attention was that the Aeron was classified as ergonomic. He had
thought the Aeron was only a status symbol, one heavily sought out by
start-ups that wanted the appearance of stability, not that it was a chair
to alleviate back and shoulder pain. The names of the guys who
designed it, Chadwick and Stumpf, were in the catalog, and so was a
reference to Herman Miller, the company that manufactured the
chair. Intrigued, he looked the company up on the Web.

The Aeron chair was there with a slew of other chairs. All of Herman Miller's chairs had good ergonomics, which meant they were alternatives to his car seat. The big new chair was not the Aeron, but the Mirra chair. He had seen the chair in the DWR catalog, but it carried more intrigue on the Herman Miller Web site. Herman Miller presented the chair primarily as an ergonomic solution, with "total back support," a result of four years of research and development. When he looked back at the DWR catalog, the chair was surprisingly inexpensive, priced less than the Aeron and less than most competitors' task chairs. The next day at work, Tom filled out a work order for a Mirra chair, taking a walk on the wild side and getting it in lime green.

After sitting on the chair for a week, he had much less pain, could work longer, and could concentrate better. Sure, the chair cost almost twice as much as the chairs the company normally provided, but he was more than twice as productive. He figured he had actually made up the difference in cost in the first week alone. He had actually saved the company a fortune in terms of better quality work time at the office. Now everyone asks him about his chair—after all, it is hard to ignore the lime green—and he has evolved into being the company advocate for comfortable seating. He even eventually got his purchasing agent to start ordering directly from Herman Miller, saving some money to obtain not just ergonomics but looks. For him, the comfort was the best thing, but he also relished the fact that the chair is a conversation piece and is the best-looking chair in the office. The youngest office workers love how it looks, and the oldest workers just feel better the minute they sit down.

Over time, as Tom continued to research ergonomics and furniture design, trying to help the company achieve not just physical comfort but visual appeal as well, he found new insights into innovations and evolving objectives in the furniture design industry. For instance, he became familiar with the idea of universal design, that a number of companies are trying to design products that are universally acceptable, or at least they are careful to explain why their product is not intended for any particular group's use if that is the case.

When you order a prescription, you often get two types of tops. One is child-proof, whereas the other is actually easy to open. Neither top is universal. If you have young children, you need a child-proof lid; if you are older and have limited hand strength, you want an easy-opening lid. Possibly, some company or someone will find a way to have one lid, a universal top that achieves both objectives. But the Mirra was different. It was a chair for everyone; it was a universal design like that universal top.

Tom is one of many office workers at all levels dealing with back and repetitive stress injuries. There are now experts in ergonomics, sometimes called human-factor experts, who can design a work environment to minimize the impact of long-term task seating in the workplace. The chairs designed by the best office furniture companies are now being made available to consumers, just like the best industrial-grade butcher knives have begun to appear in consumer kitchen catalogs. As many people age, they find they need a host of new products to help them stay active and fully functional, where "fully functional" to them means that their bodies will continue to perform like 30-year-old bodies instead of 50-year-old ones. They have disposable income and are happy to part with it if it pays for products that deliver. They have no time or patience for inferior substitutes.

The Toms of the world are legion, now that baby boomers are feeling the aches of aging. While appealing to this market and the broader market of those generally seeking ergonomic support in the office environment, Herman Miller has the daunting task of continuing the success of the Aeron, one of the few office furniture pieces ever to attain the status of public sensation. By any measure, the Aeron chair has been one of the most successful office chairs in the past 50 years. Herman Miller was looking for the next big design. How do you improve on a breakthrough success and make it competitive in a tough economy? By understanding the trends laid out by Tom and converting that understanding into a product.

Designing the Mirra Chair

The Mirra chair, which debuted in the spring of 2003 at the Annual NeoCon International furniture show centered in the Merchandise Mart in Chicago, was an instant hit, winning a number of awards. It is an excellent example of global design coordination: A furniture company based in Zealand, Michigan, blended a German design team and the concept of Nike shoes while holding to a new environmental standards system developed in conjunction with William McDonough and Michael Braungart. Herman Miller had made a major commitment to work with McDonough and Braungart to make their company an environmentally friendly manufacturer. Their buildings and manufacturing facilities were environmentally responsible, and now they had a new process for designing their chairs. The end result is the latest office seating sensation in the industry, the Mirra chair. The chair design not only added a new dimension ergonomically, it also used new technology and introduced a new visual design that may have the same impact on office seating trends as the Aeron did a decade ago. The German design group Studio 7.5, working with the new environmental standards team within Herman Miller, delivered a design that continues Herman Miller's tradition of brand excellence and innovation. The chair costs less than the Aeron and Herman Miller's competition. This new chair design is starting with the same success that its predecessor had a decade ago. The Aeron also won an award at the NeoCon show when it debuted and has been reviewed and discussed by design organizations and museums across the globe. It remains to be seen whether the public will embrace the Mirra and whether sales will follow a trajectory similar to that for the Aeron.

The breakthrough idea was based on the concept that a chair should be as comfortable as an athletic shoe. When giving the project to Studio 7.5, Herman Miller had no idea what the chair would look like, but it was convinced the idea was worth researching and developing. At the same time, during the early phases of the design of the new chair, Herman Miller developed a new environmental approach to help designers ensure that material and manufacturing decisions would be the best from an environmental standpoint and that products would be designed for disassembly, reuse, and recycling. A team of two Herman Miller specialists—Scott Charon in marketing and material purchasing, and chemical engineer Gabe Wing—worked with Studio 7.5 to make sure the design would be the best possible solution environmentally.

When you look you at the chair, the first thing you notice is the form of the back support and the unique pattern of holes in the hard-molded one-piece plastic shape. Just when the competition responded to the advanced breathable mesh of the Aeron, Herman Miller introduced a new solution. The Mirra achieves a new hybrid aesthetic by combining a solid polymer back with a set of organically shaped holes to look like a cross between a butterfly and a piece of Swiss cheese. This new ergonomic aesthetic provides a viable alternative to the Aeron. The shadows projected by the profile of the shape and holes add a light and unique new visual element to the landscape of a home or office. Herman Miller had to take a risk to see whether its customers would accept this new visual style and the idea of a solid one-piece back. Herman Miller has had an uncanny instinct as a company during the past 50 years, anticipating and setting new trends in material choice, product aesthetics, and ergonomics. Under the direction of George Nelson in the 1950s and 1960s, Herman Miller introduced one new classic after another for the home and then for office seating. The designers hired by the company introduced designs using bent plywood, fiberglass, and aluminum. The designs of Nelson, Charles and Ray Eames, and Eero Saarinen set a new standard for design in the office environment. The Mirra chair continues that tradition.

When you sit on the chair, the first thing you feel is the chair back conforming to your back and the woven seat supplying a firm support for your bottom. The adjustable arms are easy to set, and the material has a slight friction that prevents your elbow and forearm from slipping, keeping your arms positioned where you set them. The best thing is that, after awhile, you stop being aware of the chair. The feeling is just like a good pair of running shoes. The design team at Studio 7.5 actually consulted with Nike when designing the chair. The design team took the perspective that your back should receive the same support as the bottom of your foot. A shoe has to flex and respond to a number of three-dimensional movements of the foot, and so does a chair in a modern office environment. The challenge with a chair is the difficulty in making a size that fits everyone. Although the Aeron does accommodate size differences with three sizes of chairs, Studio 7.5 wanted to make one back and seat to fit the whole spectrum of people. By achieving this goal, it allowed Herman Miller to have to manufacture only a one-size chair, which cuts costs on tooling, manufacturing, and inventory. This feat was accomplished by choosing a plastic material for the back membrane that, enhanced by a series of organic-shaped holes, has just the right flex to conform to different-size backs. The support of the membrane is done via a Y-bar that went through several redesigns because it originally did not meet the design team's environmental standard. The original design was made from different materials. The drive to stay true to the environmental mission led to an innovation that improved the chair's comfort and, at the same time, reduced production costs. The end result is also a chair that is 96 percent recyclable.

In this case study, we roamed far and wide to identify trends. The Mirra chair is a product that is international in scope, universal and ergonomic in design, and thoughtful in terms of material, manufacture, assembly, disassembly, reuse, and recycle. It is an exciting, contemporary new look and feel for the office landscape and costs less than the leading chair it is designed to complement in the Herman Miller stable of seating options. Herman Miller is willing to share its new cradle-to-cradle environmental furniture design method with others. The company has more than enough innovation in ergonomics, aesthetics, engineering design, and manufacture, so it can be generous with its new environmental innovation. The key trends that started this discussion are aging and associated back problems, and relevant trends ended far beyond those boundaries, touching on aspects of life relevant to every country in the world.

The art of reading trends can be learned by anyone intimately involved in developing new products. You need to learn to read the dynamic social, economic, and technological factors. Based on those factors and changes in them, what are the probable directions for new needs, wants, and desires? From those directions emerge multiple opportunities for new products. The iPod and the Mirra chair each emerged from an insightful but straightforward understanding of contemporary trends. All the innovations discussed throughout this book similarly emerged from an educated understanding of yesterday's trends.

5

DESIGN FOR DESIRE—
THE NEW PRODUCT
PRESCRIPTION

The average consumer is full of unmet and unconscious desires for a wide range of experiences. Connecting with consumers' emotions and desires will make one product more appealing than another. The right blend of emotion and basic needs drives purchasing decisions and maintains brand loyalty and integrity while fulfilling consumer fantasy. Developing a sense of delight and trust in products is at the core of pragmatic innovation for both lifestyle consumer products and more functional business products.

Rochester, NY. On June 20, 2003, at 9 p.m., Susan Vaughn took her daughter Stacy to the Barnes & Noble in the mall. It was a Friday night, so the mall was still crowded for that time of the evening. Even so, Susan was amazed at how many people were in the store, and still coming. As she walked in, someone reached out to give Stacy a plastic pair of wide-rimmed black glasses, but she turned them down. They just did not go with her witch costume. Half the store had witch or wizard costumes on. For at midnight, Harry Potter and the Order of the Phoenix would become available. The party was just getting started, and the store would be open until 4 a.m., with food, music, Harry Potter readings, and, of course, the book for sale.

The Harry Potter Phenomenon

Order of the Phoenix is the fifth book in the Harry Potter series, the escape into the world of witches and wizards through the eyes of Harry, the lovable, only slightly mischievous wizard whose parents were murdered by the evil Voldemort when Harry was just an infant and whose soul, during the murder, somehow connected with the evil one himself. The series documented Harry's progress from his first year at the Hogwarts School of Witchcraft and Wizardry, when he first found out about his roots, through each year of school, and deeper into his battle with Voldemort.

The anticipation of the fifth book was an international phenomenon. The previous four books had sold nearly 200 million copies in more than 50 languages. Nearly 10 million copies of *Order* were preprinted, and more than 6 million of those sold the first day of its release. It was the fastest-selling book ever. Susan was one of those 6 million customers. Stacy had begged her to take her to the Barnes & Noble party and prepurchase the book "in case they run out." Susan had also been looking forward to the release of the new book and had wondered how long it would take her daughter to read it before Susan got to read it.

Although targeted to ages 9 to 12, the book reached younger and much older readers. Everyone could partake in the Harry Potter phenomenon. You didn't have to be one of those who loved "fantasy" literature. Harry was, really, an ordinary boy. Everyone could sympathize with Harry's childhood as an orphan raised without love by his aunt and uncle and bullied by his spoiled cousin. It is that seemingly ordinary front to Harry that allows us all to accept without question the extraordinary part of his being a wizard. Once we accept that he is a wizard, we can partake of and enjoy all that the world of witches and wizards has to offer—Bertie Bott's Every Flavor Beans (be careful which one you try), Quidditch (a game played on brooms), giants, werewolves, dragons, screaming plants, the feasts at Hogwarts with the ghost Nearly Headless Nick, potions that really work, and the evil spirit of Voldemort. Everyone, too, wants to visit Hogsmeade and indulge in a hot butter beer! Author J. K. Rowling has designed an entire realm by integrating new experiences that readers desire with the best of what readers remember and long for in historical context, such as Victorian England and quaint villages.

One of the most interesting parts of Rowling's world is Quidditch. It is a complete game that combines elements of competitive field games such as lacrosse, cricket, hockey, and roller ball with athletes playing in the air on broomsticks. What a great innovation to take a symbol, the witch's broom that is associated with scary women in black, and turn it into a vehicle for a game that children play. The *Wizard of Oz* had immortalized the flying witch when the spinster schoolteacher on her bicycle turns into the Wicked Witch of the East during the cyclone. Rowling redefined witches on brooms as inviting playmates.

Her books have inspired girls and boys to read—not just short stories, but huge volumes—and they cannot get enough. How many parents like Susan do you know who were forced to stand in line to make sure they could get the first available copies of the latest installment? Just when kids' primary interests appeared to be digital entertainment and the Internet, Harry Potter turned them back to the printed word. There has not been a dedication of this magnitude in children reading for entertainment since dime novels about cowboys and the Wild West hit bookstores in the United States and Europe around the turn of the last century.

Form and Function

Form has usually been thought of as the envelope that encloses a technology. In some situations, the two are seamless, so the technology and the form are seen as continuous. An airplane propeller or wing is an example of blended form and function. Such examples are rare. In most cases, the internal structure or mechanism must be covered by a surface to protect consumers from the product's inner workings, which might be sensitive, dangerous, or just ugly. No one covered a horse pulling a carriage, but automobile engines had to be covered by hoods for a number of reasons.

In the best examples of form encasing function, a product's shell can be used to accomplish a number of goals. The cover of a CD player can protect the inner workings from damage or dirt, make the product easier to hold, help the person who uses it to find the controls, be made into a form using a material and color that will connect to and enhance the consumer's lifestyle, and make the product distinct in the marketplace. Even the simplest of products can be differentiated from the competition with a thoughtful addition of details. The concept of form and function is at its best when both are integrated to fulfill the complete expectations of the manufacturer and the consumer. In this case, form and function can fulfill the fantasy of the consumer and generate a profit that is sustainable and that allows the company to prosper. In the case of a propeller, the form must keep the plane in the air. Beyond that, it has little additional value. A car body must protect a customer from crashes, it must house the engine, and it must also create a visual statement that people respond to. There are a variety of airplane propellers, but all the variations are driven by function. No one would use a propeller to make a fashion statement. With a car, the statement and the function are equally important, so the form and the function must work in complement. A sports car and a van have the same basic function, but the forms vary significantly to meet the needs of the different types of consumers who buy these vehicles.

The Experience Economy

Since Pine and Gilmore's insightful book, there has been much discussion of the "experience economy."[1] To a great extent, today's consumers buy experiences. Rather than vacations that are simply observational, such as traditional trips to Europe, recent years have witnessed increasing interest in participatory excursions such as backpacking in the Himalayas. Rather than just purchases of nondescript coffee in generic white cups, coffee consumption now entails carefully crafted purchase environments and containers, not to mention the new quality levels demanded of the liquid itself. Consumers are increasingly interested in the experiences that accompany products and services, in being personally engaged.

Consumer demand for experience is part of an evolution of the marketplace and of society. In an agrarian society, microeconomies at the household level produced and sold commodities. Food and clothing were goods created from commodities, put together in-house. As the industrial age replaced the agrarian, manufactured goods replaced the homespun. Food and clothing looked homespun but were mass-produced. Diners, for instance, served the same foods that were served in homes, but on a larger scale. As the service industry has grown to be a major portion of Gross Domestic Product (GDP), it has added its own unique value to the marketplace. Chefs created new blends of commodities, and food no longer mimicked the homemade. The fashion industry reinvented clothing. Now that consumers

1   Pine, B. J., II, and J. H. Gilmore. *The Experience Economy*. Harvard Business School Press, Boston, 1999.

are moving beyond simple services to experiential purchases, not only do consumers at Asian restaurants manipulate chopsticks rather than knife and fork, but restaurants such the Rain Forest Café have emerged that imitate the environment of South American rainforests, or at least what people want them to look like. Clothing fabrics, such as Eliotex, speak of outdoor adventure even while worn comfortably indoors. Of course, this progression applies far beyond food and clothing to other product spheres. Lawn care? Homeowners who once replaced their lawn mowers with lawn services now use professional landscapers to achieve outdoor gardens of bygone castle eras.

The Fantasy Economy

When Thomas Jefferson penned the goals of the United States as "life, liberty, and the pursuit of happiness," he set into motion one of the most powerful engines of change in the history of the world. Two hundred and thirty years later this objective has been adopted as a global mantra.

Now that China has joined the world of economic freedom, the overwhelming majority of the earth's population feels entitled to live in pursuit of the themes that Jefferson established as a basis for the founding of the United States. The end of communism and the overthrow of dictators around the world have increased the potential of individuals to achieve a life where liberty is a basic right. People have more freedoms than ever before and, as a result, more options to choose from.

The increase in global consumption has driven the pursuit of desire, or fantasy, to achieve everyone's personal sense of happiness. Not only has this pursuit altered the direction of life, for the concept of life itself is being understood as never before, but life itself has simultaneously been extended, for the average life span has almost doubled from the time when Jefferson lived. To meet this new global demand, companies now have the goal of developing innovative products and services.

Fueled by global communication of information, infotainment, and pure entertainment, individuals around the world have access to the latest changes and emerging ideas, and change occurs with an ever-quickening pace. What is the next step in the progression from commodity to good to service to experience? In our view, it is fantasy. Fantasy, according to one definition,[2] serves the purpose of fulfilling a wish or psychological need. People not only want to experience their environment, they also want to project their environment and their emotions about that environment to a deeper level of desire. They do not want to just participate in the experience; they want to live it. They already live one experience—the reality of their own lives. Fantasy is a desirable experience that, at least currently, is not that reality.

Consumers are adept at life in realms outside their own reality, at times more comfortable in a fantasy realm than in reality. Individuals converse using movie imagery. Video games, an $11 billion industry, allow consumers to interact with and even control the fantasy realm. Disney World is more than an experience; it is a fantasy for every child and adult. You can stay in the Wilderness Lodge at Disney World and not only experience the simulated Great Northwest, complete with Aaron Copland music always playing in the background, but also fantasize about living it.

In the meantime, the definition of reality itself is being changed via "reality television," where participants live for the short term in undesirable circumstances in hopes of a substantial prize. With such a definition of reality, an awkward and nightmarish world if we were confined to it, fantasy by contrast becomes all the more normal. In a post-9/11 society, people project a fantasy in which terrorist threats no longer drive reality. Even the world's money is increasingly virtual, unreal. Consumers spend money they do not have, and virtual markets exist with individuals buying and selling on the Internet with virtual PayPal accounts. Even at an international level, virtual money

---

2 *The American Heritage Dictionary of the English Language* (taken from www.dictionary.com).

passes between countries in stupendous volumes in almost no time. As reality becomes more challenged and as people come to expect a more desirable experience, fantasy becomes the driver of product and service purchasing—for this is the fantasy economy.

Fantasy in Everyday Products

Product developers today understand this evolution in purchasing expectation. It has transitioned from the entertainment industry to any industry where people interact with a product or service—not only consumer products, but industrial and business-to-business as well. One consumer company that exemplifies the motto of form and function fulfilling fantasy, in each of its 500 products, is OXO International. OXO's first product, the popular GoodGrips vegetable peeler, has received extensive publicity. The product was envisioned by Sam Farber, whose wife had arthritis in her hands. She found it difficult to use the typical 100-year-old peeler design and most other kitchen utensils, but she loved to cook. Whereas younger consumers may not see the ability to hold a product comfortably as a fantasy, many arthritis suffers do. They long for the time in life when simple things, such as opening jars or waking up without pain, were something you took for granted. Farber's peeler was an unexpected entrance into the world of kitchenware. The large oval handle made from neoprene provided an easy-to-grip shape and surface for those with less grip strength. The patented fin pattern provided added grip when the handle was wet (and was a unique aesthetic that became the product's brand identity). The improved blade required a blade guard that added visual substance and balance to the overall design. The product cost five times its traditional competitor, the designed-for-manufacture metal peeler that had been the standard design for the past century. Yet the peeler, originally designed for people with arthritis, met the needs of the growing societal trends toward improved aesthetics within refurbished kitchen environments. Soon, the GoodGrips became a mainstay for all kitchens, and all people, young and old.

The GoodGrips led to a revolution in kitchenware from an aesthetic or style perspective, but also from the perspective of comfort and usability. The idea of great-looking products that could be used by people of different needs became the company's identity. Today, OXO has more than 500 products, all designed with the goal of universal design. In other words, anyone who should be able to use the product will be able to do so, as with the Mirra chair featured in Chapter 4, "Identifying Today's Trends for Tomorrow's Innovations." OXO has received numerous design awards, including a Gold Design of the Decade award from the Industrial Designers Society of America (IDSA) and *Business Week*. OXO, which began as just a vegetable-peeler company, was bought in mid-2004 by Helen of Troy for $275 million.

Every product that OXO makes competes against mature products. Yet each of the 500 products designed by the company is a unique innovation, usually focused on usability and aesthetics. In other words, every innovation from OXO is an extraordinary part of the ordinary. Each product—a vegetable peeler, a salad spinner, a measuring cup, a dustpan and brush—has well-established overall functionality. But the way that the functionality is met through its design is extraordinary, unique, and an improvement over the state of the art.

Consider what some regard as OXO's best product—its salad spinner. Traditional salad spinners are bowls with colander inserts and a cover that meshes with the colander and enables the colander to spin through a crank mechanism on top. The user turns the crank with a rotational motion of the arm while pulling the crank knob, and the spinning colander then throws the water off the lettuce and into the bowl, thus drying the lettuce and inviting your favorite salad dressing to stick to the dry green leaves. The problem is that the motion and effort to make the colander spin is difficult for some and cumbersome for all.

OXO's innovation came from the desire to have a person use a simple one-handed motion to cause the colander to spin. The insight came from children's toys where a pump on top of a clear plastic dome causes the dome within to spin, providing the means for images to rotate and colored balls inside to jump over bumps on the base. OXO figured if a two-year-old can use one hand to get a bowl to rotate and balls to jump, the same mechanism could allow an adult to spin a colander to dry lettuce.

The result is a beautifully executed design. The black neoprene knob on top stores flush and pops up for use. A smooth vertical motion inputs the user's energy into the system. The knob's color and form contrasts with a white top and colander within a clear bowl. The colander and bowl work to provide minimal friction during spinning. The form is well thought out, with the colander having a refined rectangular mesh pattern that completes the clean look of the overall product, making it attractive enough to store on the countertop rather than hide in a cabinet.

Another one of OXO's products, the measuring cup, has an angled surface that allows you to look down at a partially filled cup to see exactly how much liquid is stored within. The extraordinary part of the design, the innovation, came from identifying the difficulty and frustration that people have with needing to level a cup, at eye level, while filling it to see how much liquid is being added. Since its inception, OXO has sold more than $9 million worth of these measuring cups.

Even OXO's simple dustpan and brush provide a superior means to sweep up crumbs off the floor. Its bristles flow out from an ergonomic egg-shaped handle that encourages a natural and effective sweeping motion. The handle also provides the means to wedge the brush into the dustpan's handle for easy storage and to make sure that the two don't get separated and lost, a frustration with other designs. The side of the dustpan is molded with teeth that serve as a means to clean the brush, another frustration with competitive products.

Many of these innovations have been patented. They all brilliantly execute their functions. The vegetable peeler easily and comfortably peels, and the brush and dustpan efficiently work in concert for dirt removal. They also beautifully express an appropriate aesthetic. If on display in a modern kitchen, any of them would make the kitchen look even better. All of these provide not just an experience, but fantasy.

Form and Function Fulfilling Fantasy

Fantasies take place on a personal level, in that individuals create fantasy. A product can support and even engender the fantasy, but the fantasy is that of the individual. It is like seduction, in which the seduced is a willing partner. Humanity has canonical fantasies; we have collective dreams. We dream of adventure, of independence, of security, of sensuality, of confidence, and of power. To achieve a sense of adventure, products promote excitement and exploration. To achieve the feeling of independence, products provide freedom from constraints. For security, products provide a feeling of safety and stability. For sensuality, products provide a luxurious experience. For confidence, they support the user's self-assurance and promote motivation of product use. For power, products promote authority and control.

The OXO vegetable peeler, through its ergonomics, gives older users the ability to work comfortably, which is independence. Along similar lines, it supports their health, touching on security. Because the product works so easily and efficiently, it promotes their confidence in daily tasks—confidence that tends to be eroded as people age. Although these everyday tools are not luxurious relative to jewelry, they are luxurious relative to other kitchen tools, providing sensuality.

How does this vegetable peeler foster fantasy for a broad market? It is simply that the experience it provides exceeds the reality of the typical user. A young buyer does not have luxury throughout the house, so a luxurious vegetable peeler speaks to the fantasy of a life of luxury. Elderly buyers' physical mobility constrains their tasks, and the ease with which they implement this peeler speaks to their fantasy of independence.

How is fantasy put into a product? What elements of a product induce users to fantasy? Customers expect a product to enhance and fulfill their lifestyle, not simply to perform a function or even to exhibit a desirable aesthetic. When a product fulfills fantasy, it fulfills a desired lifestyle beyond, and in contrast to, the current reality. In this book, the methods and tools support the development of fantasy-enriched products and services. The products and services fulfill some level of fantasy in their users, and the companies and product developers understand the paradigm of the fantasy economy. They drive successful product development under the mantra that form and function fulfill fantasy.

The Harry Potter Fantasy

Harry Potter is a great example of a product for which form and function fulfill fantasy. Almost all products are accompanied by a service, and the Harry Potter series is no exception. Although the creation of the book prose itself is relatively straightforward, coming from the mind of a single product designer, J. K. Rowling, a vast production and distribution system prints, ships, and sells the product. For bookstores, the book brings in people who are likely to purchase other books, or to drink a latte at the café. The book also has the same positive impact on Web-based retailers (minus the latte), where recommendation agents tempt purchasers with additional options and where delivery is an additional service. Because of the popularity of the Harry Potter series, *Order of the Phoenix* could be preordered months in advance on Amazon.com with the promise of quick delivery at a discount.

Beyond the book and the services that accompany it, Harry Potter has created an industry. Merchandizing has led to products including multiple computer and video games, Lego games, sunglasses, Bertie Bott's Every Flavor (Jelly) Beans (of course), and even Harry Potter cologne. The books have led directly to the production of movies. The first three Harry Potter movies each grossed around $90 million in the first weekend of their release. To date, they are three of the top six movies in terms of gross receipt their first weekend, each grossing more than $250 million over time.

The movies, themselves an entertainment service, have stayed true to the spirit of the books. They are accessible to the young and old. Like the books, they are an escape into the world of wizards and witches. Rowling's rich writing is as descriptive and captivating as the movie set. The connection of the movies to the Harry Potter stories, which everyone fantasizes about being a part of, have allowed for an exceptional cast, each supporting the mystique of Harry's world.

The Harry Potter movies are an interesting contrast to the Dr. Seuss movie *The Cat in the Hat*. Dr. Seuss books, written for readers and soon-to-be readers who are younger than the Harry Potter reader, have brought smiles to children for the past 70 years. The books stimulate children's imaginations while teaching them the magic of words. Although some of the characters are slightly naughty, they are never bad, crude, or mean. The message of Dr. Seuss was lost in the movie *The Cat in the Hat*, which featured the industry of Mike Myers as a rude and crude Cat in the Hat. The technology was there, but the translation was a dismal failure. Rowling approved the translation of her books into movies, but unfortunately (or fortunately for him), Dr. Seuss did not live to see his book translated. The movie was largely panned and, although not a complete financial failure, likely because of the fans of Mike Myers, the film appears to have barely broken even through theater distribution (although video sales will probably bring the studio a fair profit). In contrast, the third Harry Potter movie, *Harry Potter and the Prisoner of Azkaban*, which remained true to the Harry Potter themes, made a hearty profit in the just the first weekend.

If you look for other writers of fantasy with a clear English heritage, J.R.R. Tolkien comes to mind. With his extensive background in the mythologies of ancient cultures, Tolkien crafted a world of characters and dramatic contexts for *The Lord of the Rings*, released in 1954. Tolkien used his knowledge of geography to make an imaginary kingdom with subcultures that reflect ideal settings for epic adventures. Tolkien went so far as to create his own language, merged from different ones, and the theme of the search for the ring was modeled from ancient myths. This was a brilliant literary achievement and one of the best-selling books of the twentieth century, yet *The Lord of the Rings* did not flourish into mainstream until pirated paperbacks appeared in the United States in 1965. The success of *The Lord of the Rings* then quickly grew from a grassroots movement into cult status.

Although *The Lord of the Rings* movies that were introduced in 2001 were blockbusters and included an Academy Award for best picture for *The Return of the King*, the first attempts in the 1970s to make a movie based on the *Rings* trilogy did not have broad-based appeal. They were animations, most likely because special-effects capabilities were too primitive to effectively capture the story.

So the social, economic, and technological (SET) factors for the *Rings* trilogy were not as aligned as the SET factors for Harry Potter. Both the Potter books and films were instant mainstream hits with children and adults around the world because the social aspects of the story and technological aspects of the films were perfectly aligned with cultural and market demands. Although both were economic blockbuster successes in the end, it took more than a decade for the *Rings* books to grow in popularity and nearly 50 years for the movies to strike, whereas for Harry Potter, both were instantaneous hits. That is the lesson for product development. If you are developing a product in today's fast-paced world, you do not have the luxury of waiting a decade for your product to reach the tipping point to become mainstream.

The story behind J. K. Rowling and her writing of the first Harry Potter book, *Harry Potter and the Sorcerer's Stone*, is itself inspiring. A divorced mother who was on the dole in Edinburgh, England, Rowling would bring her baby in a stroller into a coffee shop and would write while her baby slept. Rowling, whose 2003 earnings surpassed even those of Queen Elizabeth, at present lives in a castle and is now one of the most recognized women on the planet. Although Rowling's success is clearly literary genius, her accomplishment is a lesson in innovation for all. Envisioning the extraordinary part of the ordinary, a wizard's blood-line in an ordinary-looking boy, was the kernel of her success. For each of us, all that is ordinary holds the possibility of the extraordinary.

Harry Potter serves as a metaphor for innovation in product development. Finding a way to make the ordinary into something extraordinary is a key lesson in product innovation. Sam Farber, of OXO, is a J. K. Rowling of new product development, taking the ordinary peeler and transforming it into an extraordinary kitchen utensil.

Fantasy-Driven Products in Everyday Experiences

It is easy to see the fantasy in the Harry Potter series. In the fantasy economy, however, fantasy can be fulfilled in the midst of everyday experiences, for fantasy is just a wish or desire. Another ordinary product is the bicycle. The basic design and function of today's bicycle is more than 100 years old. Yet the desire for improved performance on the racecourse for that added edge and the increased feature comfort for families on excursions have both driven new innovation. In each case, an unobvious aspect of the bicycle riding experience has improved the obvious design.

Trek is a company that for 25 years has pushed the innovation edge on bicycles for both the serious racer and the casual rider. Trek has used emerging composite materials technologies to reduce

weight coupled with functional innovation to improve ride performance and comfort. For example, Trek did not invent shock
absorbers for bikes, but its "fuel" suspension system better reduces
bobble and sway and its "liquid" frame design adapts the bike's geom-
etry to maintain weight distribution toward the rear tire for better
control. Most recently, the company has embraced industrial design
as a means to emotionally bridge the gap between the company and
the end users. The new sculpting in conjunction with engineering
performance has provided an identity built on performance and fulfillment of user expectations.

Lance Armstrong is very much a model of Harry Potter. Raised
in Plano, Texas, he overcame a troubled family life and pedaled his
way to becoming the record six-time winner of the grueling Tour de
France.[3] Along the way, he also became a cancer survivor, furthering
his mystique of greatness.

Trek has gained international recognition through its sponsorship
of Armstrong. Armstrong's relationship with the company goes deeper than Tiger's or Michael's or Kobe's with Nike and others, who just
use sponsors' products, maybe even exclusively. Armstrong is an integral connection to Trek's brand, and, as such, Trek has become an
advocate for cancer research. Although the Trek brand will maintain
strength without Armstrong, the long-term relationship has strong
brand association with the public. The connection predates
Armstrong's amazing world record, yet the long-term association has
propelled Trek to the forefront as Armstrong became the wizard of
bicycle racing.

Starbucks is the prototypical company that took a commodity,
coffee, and transformed it into a high-value experience at high margins. Everything about Starbucks shows success: from the coffee
itself—Arabica beans carefully obtained from select growers worldwide—to a roasting process that provides consistent flavor, to the
brewing process, to the store environment that is a cross between a

3   Wasch, H. "Armstrong cycles hope across the miles." ESPN.com, 2004.

high-end European café and an inviting college coffeehouse, to all the coffee-related accessories you can purchase as gifts for others or self. Starbucks as a service provider is the Hogsmeade of Harry Potter, and its coffee the hot butter beer, both ultimate experiences that support fantasy.

Although Starbucks is still on a rapid expansion curve, CEO Howard Schultz recognized that the growth potential for coffee consumption and new store placement are limited. Rather than wait until that limit is reached, he wanted to begin to explore new ways to grow while maintaining the company's guiding principles. Schultz read the social, economic, and technological trends. He understood the trend in music laid out in Chapter 4. He also understood the sociological connection between sophisticated coffee tastes and sophisticated music tastes. Schultz stumbled upon the Hear Music retail store. He immediately loved its service-based approach to music. Customers could buy sophisticated, unusual music and call on the educated staff to help out not just with the transaction but also with music selection, much like the service provided to patrons of an intimate wine store. Rather than commoditizing itself with shelves of ubiquitous popular top-40 hits, the store is known for hard-to-find adult-oriented music, specialty R&B, and jazz. Hear Music reaches a larger market than its target, the affluent 25- to-50-year-old who listens to NPR. The music-shopping experience at Hear Music met the coffee-buying experience at Starbucks!

Schultz believes in organic growth, so the story continues. Not only did he buy the business, he made one of its founders, Don MacKinnon, his VP of music and entertainment. He didn't just keep the business separate; he began to merge and integrate. First, Starbucks sold compilation CDs of various artists made by Hear Music. Then, Schultz and MacKinnon created a new model for coffeehouses. Customers can get their double mocha nonfat grandé latte and sit at a music station where they have access to tens of thousands of songs. As they select their menu of music as eclectic as their coffee selection, they design their own CD. They pay per song, and the

CD is burned and personalized with a CD label and jewel case insert that they select. They walk out with their half-drunk coffee and personalized CD in five minutes. The Hear Music Coffeehouses have so far been a hit, and expansion has begun, much like the initial expansion of Starbucks itself.[4]

From wizards to vegetable peelers to bikes to coffee, innovation is found by identifying the extraordinary part of the ordinary. Innovation is not wizardry or luck, but is the flower of diligent work—work that uncovers the potential that a product can achieve for its users. Harry Potter is a wonderful example of converting the ordinary into the extraordinary. Every product and service highlighted in this book is an example of meeting or exceeding the customer's emotional expectation, of form and function fulfilling fantasy. As long as those four Fs drive what you do you in planning, researching, developing, and executing your product, you will set the bar for innovation in your own field. You will deliver a product or service in the fantasy economy.

4 Overholt, A. "Thinking Outside the Cup." *Fast Company*, Issue 84, July, 2004 p. 50.

6

THE POWERS OF STAKEHOLDERS—PEOPLE FUELING INNOVATION

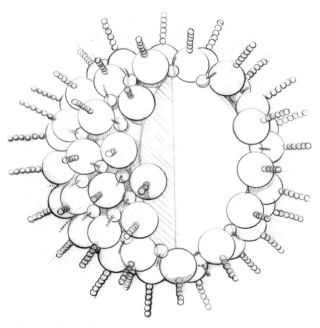

Companies know that the customer is central to product development. But it is not enough to design for the customer, because sometimes the most removed stakeholder with the least perceived power can have a significant impact on the product's success. The Powers of 10 analysis helps product developers identify all relevant stakeholders and proactively account for their needs, wants, and desires.

Houston, TX. Pete was finishing his shift, taking his bus back to the parking and maintenance area. He had driven buses in Houston for 15 years and, for the most part, enjoyed a job that some might consider monotonous. Every day seemed somewhat different, with the almost infinite variations of traffic jams and the truly infinite variety of passengers. At times, he thought of leaving the company, considered driving delivery trucks or maybe buses for another company. But driving was his life. At some point or another during his career, he had driven just about every type of vehicle with a diesel engine. Being a driver did have its downside. Pete's life was great as long as he was out on the streets, away from the boss. The office guys—the managers—didn't respect the drivers, and Pete couldn't believe he had put up with it for 15 years. Most of the guys worked hard; they spent long days not just driving, but also taking care of their buses, making sure they were clean and full of fuel and bringing them in for maintenance. It seemed that every time Pete brought his bus in for unscheduled maintenance, the boss would grill him on everything he did wrong to cause the problem. All the drivers knew that they should use extreme caution to never let water into the fuel tank (for example, when they have to fill up the tank in the rain). One guy got fired for that one.

But Pete's company recently purchased a new fuel mixture called PuriNOx that encapsulates water molecules into the fuel. Unlike adding water to a tank that mixes diesel with water, the water is actually encapsulated into the fuel in a way that it can be released when the fuel combusts. Doing so removes most of the particulates and nitrous-oxide emissions from the exhaust. But Pete did not understand that. What he knew was this new fuel looked white, like milk. Now, after all the years of telling him to keep the tank free of water, he is being forced to add the "fuel with water" to his tank.

Milan, Italy. Antoinette was frustrated about the growing level of pollutants in the air around the city. A mother of three, she worried about the health of her children. She frequently found herself angry when the bus came and she watched the black diesel fumes engulf the bus as it left for school. Antoinette saw an article in the newspaper *Corriere della Sera* that mentioned the new "Q White" fuel that the buses would be using. Q White burned cleaner and removed harmful pollutants from the exhaust. Although she originally doubted there could be such a simple solution, she was thrilled to watch the bus pull from her stop the next week. As she watched it leave, the usual black plume was replaced by a clear steam. Antoinette found herself almost gleeful that her kids were riding off to school. Of course, she would miss them, but at least now she knew they weren't being exposed to the noxious, black diesel fumes.

Lubrizol—from Technology to Product

PuriNOx, sold in the United States, and Q White, sold in Italy by Kuwait Petroleum Italia SpA (KPIT), are the same product under a different name. Scientists at Lubrizol, a company based in Cleveland, Ohio, developed this innovation in diesel fuel. Since its founding in 1928, Lubrizol has invisibly and profitably provided solutions for the oil and transportation industry. Like BASF, it didn't make the fuel; it made the fuel better. Its oil company customers came to Lubrizol with problems, and it provided solutions. It was a closed, profitable, and noncompetitive loop. Lubrizol did not have a marketing department; it did not need an ad agency or brand experts to name its products. Nor did it have to deal with competition for shelf space in a competitive point-of-purchase retail environment. It had a seamless partnership with oil companies and the transportation industry equipment manufacturers. Then, things started to change. The well started to dry up in the 1990s, and profit projections started to look like one long, continuous plateau. This was after decades of continual growth. The competition from companies that underbid its products and services and the slowing of the economy had turned a positive, predictable business into one that had a flat growth projection.

The management at Lubrizol was faced with two real options. One was to consider the safe status quo, a path that would limit growth. Or they could become a consumer-driven company built on innovation and organic growth, looking at the saturation of their current product line as an opportunity rather than as a problem.

Like many technology-oriented and successful companies, Lubrizol was fortunate enough to have resources in hand to drive organic growth. Some companies have grown by buying other companies, but utilizing existing resources offered an attractive strategic alternative and did not require the large investment needed for acquisitions. If Lubrizol was going to continue to grow, it would have to grow by becoming its own center of innovation. It could no longer rely on oil customers and the transportation industry to bring opportunities to its door. Moreover, Lubrizol recognized that it already had cutting-edge skills in an area with high growth potential, creating technology to reduce or eliminate the negative environmental impact of fossil fuels. It decided to pursue a course that would focus on bringing its technical expertise to bear on an environmental solution that would help it grow organically, from within.

Lubrizol looked back to its heritage, when the founders discovered an unmet need in the auto industry. The first product in 1928 was end-customer-driven and appeared in gas stations and auto stores all over the United States. It helped lubricate squeaky suspension systems and made lower-priced cars quieter to ride in. It was not until after World War II that the company distanced itself from the lubricant end consumer and earned its profits by supplying chemical additive solutions to the lubrication problems of the Big Three automakers, other equipment manufacturers, and the major oil companies.

Throughout the latter part of the twentieth century, Lubrizol's rich base of highly educated and, at times, brilliant research staff was given the charge to invent new but relevant technologies. More recently, chemical engineer Deborah A. Langer and her colleagues became alchemists, inventing a technique to mix oil and water.

Although it wasn't exactly gold from lead, it was significant because everyone knows that oil and water do not mix. This patented technology would provide the basis for many products that had previously been unable to take advantage of the moisturizing qualities of water. It was known that if water could be combined with fuel, it removed particulates and nitrous oxide (NOx) from the combustion process. The problem was, as Pete the bus driver knew, you cannot just pour water into an engine and hope it burns properly. Instead, it typically clogs and breaks down the engine. What Langer figured out was a process to shred and encapsulate the water molecules into the diesel fuel. When the diesel burned, it passed the water through as well, providing a clean burn while still producing sufficient BTU output. Nothing could be more innovative than developing a method for blending water and oil—the two things that are never supposed to mix. Nothing could be more valuable than reducing the output of NOx and particulates from internal-combustion diesel engines.

To take advantage of this new technology, the company put together a team whose mission was to transform the technology into a product. The team included Robert T. Graf, Ph.D., research manager; Daniel T. Daly, Ph.D., technology manager of fuels and two-cycle additives; John A. Mullay, Ph.D., principal research scientist; and Langer, principal engineer and project manager of emulsified fuel technology. What they would find out is that it takes more firepower than good chemists and engineers to meet the needs of this opportunity. It would take powers of different magnitude and scale to turn a habit of a century of diesel pollution into a neutral environmental impact.

Product developers often focus on the aspect of the product closest to their comfort zone. Technologists tend to focus on the technology alone, and technology-driven companies often believe that "if you build it, they will come." Here was a situation where the products benefits were clear. Burn this new fuel mixture in your system, and you reduce pollutants. There is no need to modify your engine to use it, so what could be the downside? Companies often fail to take into account all the different views and requirements of all the stakeholders who are impacted by their product. They fail to consider the potential difficulties in gaining market acceptance. They do not realize that end users like Pete can cause an otherwise successful product to fail in practice just because he has been taught that water in diesel is bad. They also fail to take advantage of other stakeholders like Antoinette and her enthusiasm for the product and her potential role in encouraging its adoption to protect her children. Knowing how to identify all relevant stakeholders and take into account and leverage their needs, wants, and desires is the lesson of this chapter and is illustrated by this particular Lubrizol innovation.

The Lubrizol research team developed PuriNOx, a new diesel fuel for buses and other on-highway diesel fleets. The team soon learned that despite being a great technical innovation, PuriNOx did not sell itself. Sometimes, the most removed stakeholder with the least perceived power can have significant impact on a product's success. Historically Lubrizol did not need to worry about end users. They were considered more remote stakeholders. The company had only two stakeholders that mattered: the oil companies, and the auto companies and other transportation-equipment manufacturers. The oil companies worked with Lubrizol and paid the company to invent additives to maximize performance in engines, transmissions, axles, and other power units. The auto companies and other transportation equipment manufacturers supplied hardware systems through new vehicles. Lubrizol additive products were practically invisible to end customers, distributors, and society in general. The challenge now was to redirect the team, to inspire them to become customer-driven in a new way, and to start seeing the end consumer as a key customer.

Commercialization of PuriNOx came with three challenges; two were anticipated, and the other was not. The first anticipated problem was the need to use 1.2 gallons of PuriNOx for every gallon of diesel. This reduced the range that vehicles could travel between fill-ups because they would have to obtain fuel from a central location.

The benefits of PuriNOx seemed like a fair trade-off for the reduced range, but this disadvantage made the new fuel less attractive to potential customers. The second anticipated problem was cost. There was an added price for mixing water with oil, for reducing pollutants and helping the environment. It cost 25 percent more per equivalent gallon, taking into account the greater volume of PuriNOx to diesel. But with increased pressures on companies to improve the environment and the government providing tax benefits for those who use technology to reduce pollutants, the additional cost seemed to be justified. The third problem was unforeseen—the problem of Pete's reaction and those of other end users. Although Lubrizol chemical engineers did not mind that the water-oil mixture created a white liquid instead of one with the familiar diesel color, the drivers and maintenance staff did. When these workers, many in the union, were told that there was water in the milky white substance, it elicited a strong and unexpected reaction. There was no way they should be using this fuel! They were told pretty much from birth that water has the potential to foul up an internal-combustion engine. In one test city, several bus drivers were so annoyed at being told to "put water in their tank" that they protested by urinating in the tanks! It took the evidence that the engines actually ran cleaner with PuriNOx to finally calm down these union men. They had to see it with their own eyes. Lubrizol had jumped into the world of complete product solutions, into the world where a vast number of stakeholders really did matter.

The issues at Pete's company were not ones that Lubrizol traditionally considered. Having to address the union problems and dealing with the unexpected reaction of the drivers almost ruined its product launch. Lubrizol could have minimized these issues if only it had identified them in the first place. Lubrizol could have educated Pete and other drivers on the difference between this fuel and the one he was used to. Lubrizol could have explained why the water performs differently with this technology and how using this product would improve the environment at no cost to them. Fortunately, this problem was seen early in the launch of this product, and the company was able to communicate with and educate the end users. In the end, the company succeeded in introducing this innovation into U.S. communities such as Houston, Texas, and Los Angeles and Sacramento, California. Internationally, PuriNOx was also successfully introduced into London, England, as well as Milan, Genoa, and Sicily in Italy.

The Lens of *Powers of 10*

The key to understanding the impact of immediate and remote stakeholders is to understand the power of product adoption from the smallest (micro) to largest (macro) view—to identify stakeholders affected by each view and to understand the impact of the product based on that view. We developed a technique to identify such a broad range of stakeholders in the context of a product, a technique that we call a "Powers of 10" analysis. The name and inspiration came from the film *Powers of 10*, produced by Charles and Ray Eames. They were a husband-and-wife team and two of the most influential designers of the twentieth century. Their furniture designs from 50 years ago are still considered some of the best today, from airport seating to the famous Eames lounge chair. They also produced more than 120 films for various companies such as Polaroid and IBM.

Powers of 10 was produced for IBM in 1977 for internal presentation to highlight the possibilities of metric scaling. The film is an 8-minute, 47-second summary of the known universe, from the smallest particle to the largest view of the galaxies, looking at what happens every time you magnify or reduce the same view by a power of 10. The film begins with an image of a couple resting in a Chicago park next to Soldier Field after having a picnic. The camera zooms back every 10 seconds, increasing the view of the scene by an order of magnitude. First, the image is of the couple, then the park, then a section of Chicago, then a section of the Great Lakes, and then the country, globe, solar system. Eventually, the earth is viewed from the distance of a light year, and the camera view continues outward through clusters of galaxies until, at 10^{24} power, the movie stops, showing a macro-cosmic view of the known universe.

From the known universe, the camera begins to quickly zoom back down through each power until the hand resting on the stomach of the man at the picnic is seen. The movie slows, and every 10 seconds, the field of view decreases by a power of 10. First, one views the skin on the hand, then the inner layer of cells, on down to molecules of neutrons and protons, and finally down to 10^{-16}, the smallest known particle in the universe at that time, the nucleus of an atom of a cell on the hand of the man at the picnic.

This vivid film quickly gives us a perspective of our place on the earth and in the universe, raising questions about our own context and role in the universe, questions that we normally might not voice but often ponder. Similarly, insightful product developers understand the role and benefits of developing a product in small-to-large relative contexts. Scientists often focus on their own small piece of the puzzle, understanding the physics and mechanics behind the atomic structure. Meanwhile, technologists focus on the machines, or components of machines, that cause the chemical reaction to take place. Consistently successful product developers understand not only the product's molecular- and machine-level context, but also the influence of the product on the people who use it and those affected by its use. In that sense, insightful product developers perform a Powers of 10 analysis, from a micro to macro view of stakeholders and the context of product use. A Powers of 10 analysis helps them anticipate where their strategic advantages are and where their potential pitfalls lie.

Powers of 10 in Action

To help Lubrizol understand the Powers of 10 view of a product and the stakeholders affected by that view, we worked with Lubrizol as it developed a new product for refineries based on the PuriNOx technology. The technology itself is the same, the same basic approach of emulsifying water into oil. But innovation is required beyond the core product itself; it is also needed in the fuel's delivery system. We discussed the three product issues earlier: range, cost, and product appearance. The fourth potential problem with this technology is that the encapsulated or emulsified water in fuel can stay in suspension for only a limited period of time unless it is agitated. For diesel vehicles, the fuel mixture can be mixed off-site and delivered to the fueling station. For larger refineries, the diesel fuel and water have to be mixed on-site just prior to being burned. So the delivery of the modified fuel is quite different, requiring the development of a new product system. This new product Lubrizol called Emulsified Heating Fuel, or EHF for short.

Powers of 10 One: Molecular

The most micro view of the PuriNOx technology is the chemistry on the molecular level—the creation of water molecules that can be suspended in the oil. The way to mix water and oil is to shred or shear the water into droplets so small that they can be "hidden" in the fuel molecules. The water is actually suspended inside the diesel fuel. The people who concern themselves with the chemistry are the technologists at Lubrizol, the ones who actually invented the technology. But there are other concerned parties (for starters, the Lubrizol executives who invest in the technology and envision the product's commercial success). As mentioned earlier, historically Lubrizol has not been a marketing-focused company. It has been driven by chemical innovation and technical development. Marketing and brand identity took a backseat to the technology. Not in the case of PuriNOx or EHF, however. Lubrizol's traditional approach needed to change. The company hired an advertising agency to promote this wonderful new innovation. The first problem came when the ad agency, another stakeholder at the most micro level, looked at the molecule that was formed around water droplets, the chemistry that allowed the water to be suspended in the diesel fuel. The agency reaction was that the new molecular structure looked like one of the early sex-education movies used to show an egg being impregnated by sperm. In the agency's opinion, the smaller molecules that encapsulated the water droplets looked a lot like sperm cells! It was a toss-up as to who was more concerned about this potential comparison—the upper management of a conservative company or the ad agency afraid of the jokes that their ads might provoke. So they did what any self-respecting agency would do: They found another way to visualize the new miracle molecule.

They ended up making it look like a new type of candy with a chocolate center, a caramel second coating, and an outer coating of chocolate. It turned out to be an interesting collaboration. The ad agency was not used to promoting micro-level molecules as a product, and the company was not used to promoting itself. To make things even more interesting, the original team of chemists and inventors were not happy that their innovative complex molecule now looked like a new type of junk food. This was the first Powers of 10 challenge. Another challenge was a concern about showing too much detail regarding the construction of the molecule and the chemistry. Reveal too much, and Lubrizol could be giving away valuable trade secrets. The ad firm and technologists should have worked to tell the story about the insight that led to the innovation rather than focus on the look of the molecule itself. The answer from the Powers of 10 analysis was not to corrupt the way the molecule works but to talk about the innovation and its potential impact.

Powers of 10 Two: Blending

To properly place the modified water molecule in the oil, it must be blended in a particular way. Thus, machines needed to be designed and built to accomplish this process, adding engineers and possibly suppliers to the list of those who matter to the success of this product. This was also an opportunity to anticipate the third Powers of 10 level and to think about new opportunities and the need to establish a brand identity for the product and for the company. What form would the blending take? Would it be hidden from view or prominently displayed in a machine in the center of the refinery? The decision was the latter, requiring the development of a complete blending unit. The original plan was a gray box hiding the product and company, as Lubrizol was used to doing. But the Powers of 10 analysis indicated that this blending unit also provided the opportunity to begin establishing a visual brand identity, drawing attention to the unit and the unique product within.

Powers of 10 Three: Blending Machines

The modified water molecules can float, but not permanently; eventually, they settle to the bottom of the mixture unless they are stirred. In a refinery, the goal is to have the blending machine on-site, mixing the fuel only as it is sent to the burner. All of a sudden, there are many people who need to care about the EHF product. The key customer to Lubrizol is the plant manager and buyer who make decisions regarding the fuel (including whether to purchase it). These key customers' concerns have always been of Lubrizol's target. But there is also the person who maintains the boiler and the new mixing unit. The ability for this person, and others like him, to incorporate the new product into his work routine is critical to the product's long-term success. How will he react? Because stakeholders are real people with their own individual goals, needs, egos, and viewpoints, rich descriptions of stakeholders are used within the Powers of 10 analysis through scenarios to reveal insights into how stakeholders can facilitate or hinder the progress of new products. Anticipating stakeholders' needs affects the product design itself; companies want their products to be widely appreciated and accepted.

Consider Eric, who is responsible for maintaining several boilers in the plant. How will he react? One attribute of the product is that it can be burned by current boilers without having any retrofit. One approach the company can take is to have the refinery try out EHF on a single boiler. They can observe the burn and emissions. If they are not happy, they can just bypass it and go back to their original setup. The blending mechanism is intimidating to Eric. The chemistry is unfamiliar to him; he works with mechanical things. He is skeptical about the EHF product, and he now has one more job to do in maintaining the equipment. Does he know that maintenance is low and Lubrizol support will always be available, 24/7? Lubrizol anticipated the concerns of maintenance guys like Eric and instituted a support program that is available any time, any day. Eric is curious about the white liquid, and wouldn't believe it if he didn't see the results himself. The flame looks better than he has ever seen it burn, and the machines are clean. Eric can tell his family and friends that the plant has made an effort to be more efficient and reduce pollution that is harmful to the environment.

Powers of 10 Four: System Operation

At the next Powers of 10 level is the system-level analysis of the refinery operation, including the new blending unit. Here are the facilities planner, who makes room for the new equipment, and the person who controls the boiler that burns the fuel. Again, these people need to be considered, and the Powers of 10 analysis at this level helps us do this. Are they allies or foes? If foes, can they be turned into an advantage?

Think about Steve, a union member who has been working as a boiler operator for 20 years. He prides himself on his efficiency with his boiler. He is comfortable with the controls for optimizing fuel mixtures and knows exactly how his boiler reacts to different qualities of fuel. For Steve, switching to EHF means a loss of knowledge and a need to learn new proportions and characteristics to control the fuel. The tools for optimizing the mixing will stay the same, but efficiency will change. He will also have a new responsibility added to his daily tasks—managing the blending unit that will be installed at his station.

The management might explain that the fuel burns cleaner and is more efficient, but will Steve have trouble explaining to his family and friends why he has to burn greater quantities of fuel for the same output? (Again, as mentioned earlier, the water adds volume, so it takes more fuel for the same output, although not more diesel.) As did the bus drivers with PuriNOx, Steve talks to his peers, the other guys in the plant who are also not sure about putting water in the equipment—that, again, has always been a hard-and-fast rule. As previously mentioned, this new stuff looks like milk! Steve will do what his plant manager says to do, but he doesn't want any headaches or any problems changing over to this new product.

However, what about Steve's colleagues? Will they be as open-minded? They are members of the union. Will they complain about this change and make demands that could seriously impact the acceptance of the fuel product?

One way to address Steve and Eric's concerns is to educate them on the benefits and use of the product, not to pitch the benefits to the plant manager alone. From the start, the operators and maintainers will have a sense of the goals of the new product and the purpose behind the process changes. Also, education will help product idiosyncrasies to be less strange, more familiar. Remember, this new white stuff looks nothing like a petroleum product. The challenge is to use the white color as an advantage in establishing a brand identity for the product.

Powers of 10 Five: Community

Most companies would stop there, if they considered such a broad range of stakeholders at all. But there are more. As the Powers of 10 increase, the refinery produces particulates and NOx emissions. This affects residents around the refinery, politicians dealing with pollution in their city, and even the gas stations that sell the gas produced by the refinery. Could these stakeholders harm the product's success? Or could they be used to the company's advantage? Do they understand how many pollutants come from the refinery? Would they be willing to pay extra for their fuel if it is produced with EHF and the air that they breathe is cleaner? Not only does this power begin to address quite removed stakeholders, it also begins to indicate how politics and visibility to the public can influence the product's success.

Consider Felicia, a high-school science teacher from Boston and mother of one. She pays a lot of attention to the news, especially environmental issues. To contribute to cleaning up the environment, she uses public transportation to get to school, believing that automobiles are the leading cause of the city's pollution.

Felicia brings clippings about Boston's environmental concerns to her classroom and asks her students to bring in articles as well. This week, her class is discussing pollution because she recently read an article in the *Boston Globe* about NOx pollution and particulate matter. She had thought that cars were the major cause of pollutants, but it turned out that industrial plants were. Cleaning up the air and reducing pollution will cost money. She encourages her students to decide for themselves whether they would pay more for clean air. Felicia asks her class to write letters to representatives in Congress and to the governor as well as to executives of the refinery in their community, asking them to support initiatives that reduce pollution. Felicia and others like her are impacted by and can have impact on refineries in their communities and thus are an important part of stakeholder analyses that cannot be ignored, as highlighted by the Powers of 10 analysis.

Powers of 10 Six: Region

As the Powers of 10 increase, so does the range of their influence. This is often the power that becomes the political decision-making. If the scenarios take place in the New England area, then that area's politicians become stakeholders, as do members of environmental organizations and neighboring regions who might breathe the air that flows from New England. Will the governor want to clean up the air if doing so only means using a different type of fuel? One other political arm that might become an ally is the policymakers who examine pollution. One such organization is NESCAUM, the Northeast States for Coordinated Air Use Management. Capturing the attention of these policymakers may lead to a government subsidy for the more expensive EHF product, and may even lead to mandates for its use.

Although Felicia by herself wields little power, she may reach those who have considerable influence—someone like Deion, executive director of air quality management at NESCAUM. He received his Ph.D. in environmental policy and has worked his way up through the levels of the organization. His main task is to make proposals for regulations in the Northeast. He has earned the respect of his peers with his strong commitment to people, no matter what. Although he is adept at political maneuvering, he stays true to his ideals.

He recently learned about EHF as an alternative clean fuel. Because he works closely with industrial plants, he knows that all alternatives are costly, but this option requires little upfront capital because the current machines will not have to be replaced or retrofitted. The product offers significant and instant reduction in NOx and particulate matter.

The immediate solution of fossil fuel extension is appealing to Deion because converting to new fuels is either too far off in the future or has its own political and environmental issues. Retrofitting industrial sites with more efficient equipment is an option but has high upfront costs and takes time. Deion has the ability to look at the bigger picture, the cost of buying the EHF assembly versus other means of purifying the air. He will set up a committee to pursue the possibility of NOx credit trading with high-pollutant areas to reduce the cost of the new product to the industrial plants.

Powers of 10 Seven: Continent

At the next level is the continent, where the issues are the air in one country affecting that in another, leading to a potential increase in sales to improve air quality throughout the larger region.

Powers of 10 Eight: Global Environment

Finally, the highest power is the global environment. Problems of global warming and ozone depletion seek low-cost solutions that will have a profound impact on the human race. Might the world embrace EHF as a means to deal with this threat to humanity? This bold thought is one that the chemists and engineers who invented the product and the executives who support its commercialization might only dream of.

Scenarios Ensure That People Remain Real

The Powers of 10 analysis identifies people who are relevant, and scenarios of each of the identified individuals provide needed insight and understanding. By sketching the profile of stakeholders in scenarios, product developers can anticipate their reactions. They become real people to design for and with. The Powers of 10 analysis helps innovators identify stakeholders, envision scenarios of how their product may be used, and anticipate how it may make a difference in people's lives. It helps them think about positive influences and negative ones, and how they might design the product differently to lessen the impact of the negative ones. Designing the product includes designing the communication of the product and the services that support it; similarly, designing a service includes designing the products that support it. The Powers of 10 analysis helps the product developers understand how changing a product feature at a micro level has ramifications beyond the product itself, even impacting the experience of those who interact with it.

The important lessons from this analysis, and ones that all good product developers consider, are the extensive list of stakeholders and scenarios of their experience in using or interacting with the product or service. By considering the reaction of all stakeholders early in the process, the product developer can design solutions to potential flaws into the product itself proactively, rather than reactively after it is on the market. The cost of waiting may be negative product reviews or negative word of mouth, or the significant cost of redesigning, retooling, and remanufacturing a product—all of which can have significant impact on its bottom-line profitability.

It is always interesting to see the limited view that so many companies have of themselves. They fail to see themselves at different levels of magnitude and reduction and to understand their strengths and weaknesses. Every company should conduct a Powers of 10 analysis for its products and itself so that all product development teams understand and then reassess the charter with every new product.

In terms of Lubrizol, as the company redirects its energies to organic growth, it has dedicated itself to help make the world a better place through its fluid technologies. One way to do that is through technologies such as PuriNOx and EHF. Although Lubrizol has visions far beyond fossil fuels, it will first use its expertise to foster new growth. In 2001, *R&D* magazine recognized Lubrizol along with its project partner Caterpillar for developing one of the top 100 significant technology breakthroughs of that year. The company was particularly pleased that the award recognizes technology that significantly changes the quality of people's lives. The award was for PuriNOx and the start of a new corporate culture.

EHF currently is in front of regulators, oil company partner candidates, and end users in the Northeast United States, with an expected product introduction in 2005. EHF, PuriNOx, and any paradigm shift in a prominent industry, such as fuels, will require intense scrutiny and evidence of likely success. A Powers of 10 analysis, along with a value-driven product development process, will maximize the potential for success. Paul Basar, commercial development business manager (author of the PuriNOx and EHF business plans), says that the Powers of 10 analysis (and Value Opportunity Analysis, discussed in Chapter 9) has profoundly influenced the company's thinking in all its new product concept projects. Basar says, "The concept of looking at all players, all stakeholders, and understanding both the micro and macro view of what we are doing, is very key now in all our thought processes on new concept development."

7

B-to-B Innovation—
The New Frontier
of Fantasy

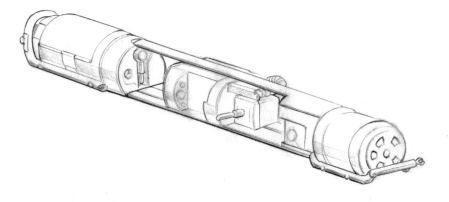

Companies in business-to-business (B-to-B) markets often look at innovation as a consumer-driven revolution and not as something that applies to them. Their primary customers have been all about price and functionality, not lifestyle and desire. Because only one company can be the cheapest and most price-driven, commoditization stifles growth; these companies must find the power of innovation. Now the same high-value user experience is starting to be expected even for business-to-business products and services. Meeting these expectations requires not simply research and development but also a thoughtful strategic plan.

Trenton, NJ. It was a evening in November. Joey Russo and his team were getting in place for a long night. They would have 12 hours to get their work done and then inspected so that the day crew could move on to the next segment of pipe. Every day, the day crew relines decaying sewer pipes. Every night, Joey and his team surgically "cut the laterals."

In every major city in the developed world, the sewers are more than 50 years old. The original piping was mostly clay-based, a material that becomes fragile and susceptible to cracking with age. Sewer pipes are typically 8 inches in diameter, too small for humans to physically enter to repair. There are two approaches to rehabbing sewer lines. The oldest is to dig up streets and yards to gain access to the pipes and replace them. This approach is prohibitively expensive and undesirable for everyone who lives in the neighborhood. The second, noninvasive procedure is to pull tools through the pipe. These tools are used to lay out a liner and then cut out the openings that connect the main pipe to the outlet to the homes, called "laterals" in the industry. The process is still essentially manual. Locations for the laterals are mapped out ahead of time, and a machine with a camera and cutting tool is then pulled through the pipe with a winch and is stopped at the locations that have been mapped. A skilled person like Joey then sits in a truck and looks at a video monitor that shows the location where the lateral is to be cut. (The liner has a dimple in it where the pipe coming into the main pipe intersects.) The person in the truck controls the cutter and watches the dim and colorless images on the monitor as he directs the machine to cut the lateral. The process is slow and tedious and takes years of experience to master, but it is instrumental to the success of the operation. Although this approach is preferable to brute-force digging, it does have its downsides. First, this expert lateral cutter demands a hefty salary (in some cases, more than $100,000). Second, this person and the equipment are the bottleneck to the speed of opening the pipes that lead to people's houses. Third, the crew has up to 12 hours to open the lateral, or else sewage backs up into the house, forcing the sewer rehabber to quickly dig up the yard and open the pipe while irate homeowners look on.

Joey is that master cutter. He is often away from home at night, but the salary is worth it. His boss, Sal, knows Joey can jump ship and go to another company at any time, so Sal has to make sure he treats Joey well. Sal is nervous because Joey is not easy to replace, and if he is sick or leaves, Sal will not be able to get the jobs done. Joey's apprentice does not have enough experience, and Joey is not interested in giving him on-the-job training to create his own competition. Even though Sal does not have to stay and direct the night crew, he often loses sleep hoping that the morning will bring a completed section of cut laterals. Sal loses a small fortune if the laterals back up because they are not cut in time. He faces crews showing up with nothing to do if the laterals do not pass inspection. His agita is so bad that it prevents him from eating his favorite foods, and his blood pressure is off the charts if he fails to take his medication. Whereas the day crew's work is important, the night crew critically impacts both the physical output of the business and its income statement.

Everyone had thought the liner technology was the perfect answer when it was invented. When he bought the business, Sal was told how much pipe could be lined and how profitable the business was. The lateral cutting seemed like a small part of the operation, with a specialized cutting tool to do the job remotely. But a large chunk of the profits go to Joey and his team. Plus, his current cutters break down all the time, so the crew has to travel with spare parts and be expert repairmen on-site. The business is really not that profitable after all. Sal would love a better pipe rehab process.

The Industrial Frontier

In one industry after another, people fantasize about the perfect product or environment. It may be the worker on the job, the manager who does not sleep at night, the family member who wishes that a spouse could return earlier and less fatigued from work, or the children who wish their parents could attend their hockey games. Sometimes, the fantasies are in direct conflict. Joey wishes he could work better hours. He is the master of his job and competition is scarce, but he is concerned about burnout. Sal wishes there were three guys who could run his lateral cutter so he could pay the operators less and reduce his cost, have more options for who is working, and rotate his crew to limit burnout. The important thing to realize is that fantasy and value expectations are now desired in the realm of business-to-business products and services. The fantasy economy has expanded from the home and into the workplace.

Jeff Calhoun, vice president of product development for laboratory equipment company VistaLabs, says that industrial products are the "last frontier" in new-product development. The B-to-B product domain in general suffers from a lack of good design, a lack of attention to the experience of use, and a general lack of connection to the user. The goal, then, is to tame the industrial frontier. To take the wild landscape of mundane and functional but undesirable technologies and transform it into an oasis of user experience, of fantasy.

Many industrial technologies are mass-produced but are usually designed and manufactured with a cost-cutting commodity mind-set. A bolt is a bolt is a bolt, so the company that makes them cheapest will sell the most. But someone will be the first to design a bolt with attention to ergonomics of use, with color codes that instantly communicate different thread sizes, and with a brand identity that associates those innovations with the company that makes them. That company will find itself with growing profits while everyone else desperately works to stay in the black by continuing to cut production costs. In other words, the form and function will create value for both the company and the purchaser.

Fantasy in Industrial Products

There are already many existing examples of industrial and business-to-business products that fulfill fantasy. Consider, for instance, the agriculture industry. What if there was an agriculture combine that not only was extraordinarily efficient at its main function but also was designed with an eye toward ease of maintenance, with easily opened panels to provide complete maintenance access along with a built-in service platform and foldaway maintenance ladder? What if its electronics were the most sophisticated in the industry, not only adapting the performance to field conditions but even including a system to identify and remove stones from the field? What if the combine looked so sleek and exciting that it seemed almost fun to drive, was comfortable to sit in, and had state-of-the-art lighting and a global positioning system? New Holland created just that combine, with an international team of American and Belgian engineers along with industrial designer Russell Strong of Integrated Vision. This combine, the CR, has won awards worldwide, such as the 2002 Gold Business and Industrial Product IDEA award, given jointly by the Industrial Designer Society of America and *Business Week* magazine.

What if a machine tool operator could just flip a lever to quickly release and change a tool bit and then flip the lever again to secure it in place? This rather than taking an Allen wrench and unscrewing each bit, replacing it, and then having to screw down the bit with the Allen wrench again. A tedious job and one that is typical in the industry, the standard approach may change due to the patent-pending ergonomic lever design by mechanical engineering students at Carnegie Mellon, working with Paul Prichard and others at Kennametal's Breakthrough Technology Group.

What if you had constant continuing education via a hands-on magazine, one that even provided samples of new materials and technologies so that you could incorporate the most cutting-edge technologies into your product? And what if you knew this because you could subscribe to such a magazine provided by the company Inventables? Every third month a technology kit called DesignAid would be delivered to your door, complete with Web support to keep you abreast of the latest developments not only by text, but also by touch and feel. Inventables is a supplier of knowledge, of the building blocks for technical innovation. Zach Kaplan and Keith Schacht, the principals, developed the company after meeting in college. Today their customers include GM, HP, and IBM. Although their main goal is to provide information for teams to use in product development, the kits have been applied in a host of different ways. For example, they are used to help to stimulate teams to think out of the box, and managers are using the kits as a creative education tool to open up individuals and teams as a warm-up exercise.

The final example considers respirator masks. In every hazardous work environment, employees need to wear respirators. The problem is many of these masks are so uncomfortable that workers often fail to comply with health and safety rules. What if workers in hazardous areas wore comfortable masks that were made to be comfortable not only during work but also during breaks? Hired by the Aearo Company, Elizabeth Lewis and her team at Product Insight, Inc. designed such a respirator, and it won the Bronze IDEA award in the same competition as the New Holland CR. Lewis, her company, and the mask are discussed further in Chapter 11, "To Hire Consultants or Build Internally—That Is the Question."

The farm machinery combine, the quick change for machine tools, the DesignAid technology kit, and the respirator mask may not seem to have the aura of Quidditch, or the Trek bike, or the OXO salad spinner, or a Starbucks nonfat double latte with a shot of caramel. But they are still examples of form and function fulfilling fantasy. The fantasy here is to have an experience that exceeds the standards of current products, beyond the reality of the industry status quo. Even on the farm, the combine provides a comfort level and an aura of a high-end office space and yacht. Even in the midst of a production tool room, the fantasy is a clean environment and effortless maintenance of the machines. Even in the midst of a rapidly changing technological world, the fantasy is continuing education that explains the complexity of the latest technological advances with the simplicity of "show and tell." Even in the midst of hazardous environments, the fantasy is the ease and comfort of a world especially designed for humans rather than opposed to them.

RedZone Robotics: Going from Projects to Products

A common business model for industrial technologies is that of one-off projects. A one-off project is a single solution made to a given specification of functional requirements within a cost constraint. These projects are means to flex technical prowess, and each one is satisfying to the team that develops it. But one-off industrial technology projects are produced by companies that typically have no brand identity, no contact with end users, and no understanding of a customer-based value proposition with attention to the experience of use. This kind of project-based company faces operational hurdles, both with the constant need for acquisition of new projects and with the internal needs to juggle people and resources to meet delivery dates. At the same time, no equity is being built. The company possess capabilities but no repeatable income stream that generates profits for company growth. This kind of company works to keep up, not get ahead.

The alternative is to focus on repeatable business and develop products and services that can be reproduced or even mass-manufactured. Here, technical prowess would translate into complete product proficiency. An example of a company that has successfully made that transition is RedZone Robotics. Previously a custom robotic project shop, RedZone robotics will be the company to resolve Sal's indigestion and high blood pressure caused by his sewer rehab company.

Founded in 1987 out of the robotics technologies developed at Carnegie Mellon University, RedZone went into Chapter 11 bankruptcy in 2002. Although RedZone's technology was state-of-the-art, its one-off project business model was not. The key words in the markets for robotic technology are "dangerous, dirty, and dull," and RedZone had especially focused on the dangerous. Prior to its bankruptcy, the company built high-profile, one-of-a-kind robots for tasks where humans could not or should not go. For example, RedZone developed robots to help clean up Chernobyl and Three Mile Island.

Current CEO Eric Close and his investors acquired RedZone Robotics while it was in Chapter 11 and brought it out of the bankruptcy process. Close says he "loves bankruptcy." He should. He has been dealing with it for nearly a decade. But he doesn't get companies into bankruptcy—he gets them out. Close is a turnaround specialist. He buys companies in bankruptcy and turns them into profitable enterprises. In his short career, he has bought four troubled companies. These companies were either on the brink of bankruptcy or already in bankruptcy when he took control of them and turned them around. According to Close, bankruptcy has its advantages, providing "great bargains" if chosen well. The problem with starting a new company is that it is hard to develop technologies, infrastructure is expensive to buy, and it is hard to get the first customer. Close says that companies in bankruptcy can get you through these first hurdles. They come with technologies that they have developed but could not turn into profitable revenue streams. They come with facilities and equipment where that technology was developed. Oddly enough, they usually have happy customers.

Happy customers may seem like an oxymoron for a company in bankruptcy. But, according to Close, these companies often have a small customer base that they have given a lot of attention to. They must, because it is their only hope for sales. Surprisingly, suppliers are not a significant roadblock either. Although some may stop doing business with the company, many are happy to maintain the account and are pleased to see new management trying to turn the business around. Even though the company has normally defaulted payment on its obligations to the supplier, most suppliers want to retain the company as a customer. If you can convince suppliers that you will be a stable customer going forward, they want to work with you.

The big problem with companies in bankruptcy is the employees. Many are disgruntled; morale is down. The culture is a negative one based on a long period of cost cutting and a stifling environment. Often, these employees may be technically talented but may not be team players. So the task is to reinvigorate the employees.

RedZone was one of these companies. Close purchased RedZone in June 2003 and became its president and CEO. The "bargain" he got was some of the most advanced robotics technology commercially available at that time. His challenge was to turn RedZone from a *project*-based company into a *product*-based company. How could he use the impressive technology basis to produce an assembly-line product, one that could be produced on multiple runs, if not mass-produced? As he searched the social, economic, and technological (SET) factors looking for trends, he realized the $120 to $200 billion possibility in sewer rehabilitation in the United States (and two times more worldwide in developed countries). More than 600,000 miles of small-diameter sewer line exists in the United States alone, and a significant percentage is more than 50 years old. The vitrified clay pipes are beginning to crumble and clog from debris and tree roots. Sewage is leaking into the environment and finding its way into streams. All that sewer line will need to be repaired in the next 40 years. This is a great opportunity for robotic technology.

Close's business plan was as good as his reputation, so he had been able to attract funding. But he had two other major challenges.

One was to motivate employees, to get everyone in the company focused in the same new direction, and the other was to make an impact in an industry completely new to RedZone. The solution for both was to connect the vision of the robotic product with the company's vision. Close wanted a product where service, product performance, and interface all smashed current industry standards, a product that would achieve fantasy status. This is the only way that sewer pipe rehabbers like Sal would leave behind existing equipment to buy the RedZone system.

The Strategic Plan

Designing a product that is so fantastic that it is beyond the status quo experience of expert users requires not simply research and development but also a thoughtful strategic plan. That plan includes three major parts: first, an understanding of who are the key stakeholders and what are their needs and desires; second, a complete product strategy that includes the development of the product and the services required to support the product through its entire life cycle of use and its interaction with its stakeholders; and third, a corporate strategy that establishes its brand and aligns itself with its products and customers.

Strategy One: Identify and Understand Stakeholders

In terms of stakeholder analysis, Close used the Powers of 10 analysis described in the previous chapter to identify and understand his stakeholders. As a result of that analysis, Close visualized the product on all levels of its functionality and recognized stakeholders at each of those levels. These stakeholders included not only owners or general contractors like Sal, and crew members like Joey, but also the inspectors of the pipes, the engineers for the communities, the politicians who set policy, and homeowners and taxpayers who are affected by the efficiency and effectiveness of the process. The scenarios that were developed for all the stakeholders made it easier for Close to see all the players as real, tangible people, like Joey and Sal. It was then clear that the product had to be easy to use, easy to learn to use, and easy to repair on-site. It was also clear that the product had to generate reports that would be easy for inspectors to review. As an outcome of the Powers of 10 analysis and scenarios, Close had a road map to show the direction in which the product and company needed to head—specifically, what the different levels and scope of the product would be, as well as the user needs for each level.

Strategy Two: Planning the Product

The next step was a micro-level analysis of the product itself, a strategy for the development of the product. RedZone's long-range product strategy is a sewer robot that will accomplish a variety of tasks. The trade-off with any multipurpose tool is accuracy for a given task. If a number of tasks, say six, need to be accomplished in sewer repair—such as inspecting the state of the main pipe, removing debris from it, lining the pipe, identifying locations where other pipes join the main line, cutting the laterals, and grouting the resulting joints—the easiest product approach would be to produce multiple stand-alone machines specifically designed to perform each task. The problem is that the customer then would need to purchase, store, and maintain each machine. At the other extreme, a single product that does it all is difficult to have as an approach to accomplish all the tasks well. Such a machine would look like something out of a Dr. Seuss book!

Rather than a line of separate machines, and rather than the Rube Goldberg approach of all in one, the solution for RedZone is a simple, robust, and powerful base machine that is the platform for multiple modules. The modules are designed to attach at a given place in a given way that each serve an individual task. The platform, loaded with a module, goes into the sewer and accomplishes one task. The platform is then removed and the first module taken off, and then the next module is placed on the platform for the next task. The core platform needs to have certain capabilities, some of which may not be used for a given task, and others that will always be used.

The product strategy is to design the platform and modules, and this strategy has implications for the product development team. The team needs to design an interface that will connect all modules to the platform. The team must understand all the capabilities the platform must have to meet the demands of each module. The physical interface for the modules must be easy to understand and use. Changing the modules will require some training for the crew, training that the RedZone team must design into the product system. The platform and the modules individually and together must be easy to manipulate in accomplishing the task. The robot platform, together with a module, must be easy to carry from the truck where it is stored, easy to manipulate through a manhole into the sewer main, and easy to remove from the sewer. It must be easy to clean and maintain. The accuracy of the tool must be at least as good as each of the individual machines available today.

Anything less than this will jeopardize the success of the product. In any established industry, it takes a true breakthrough in cost or performance to convince a market to make a change in how it performs its job. RedZone decided to improve both: decrease price, increase the speed of accomplishing the task of lateral cutting, increase the quality of the cuts, and decrease the skill level needed to accomplish the task, thus further reducing the customer's overall costs. What a task to put on a development team!

The advantage to RedZone and the only way it could meet this seemingly absurd challenge is the "bargain" that Close purchased when buying the company. RedZone has some of the world's best robotic technologies and the know-how to create new technologies to meet challenging performance conditions. RedZone has some of the best minds in the industry who, time and time again, were able to overcome technical challenges to design and manufacture machines that few others could have created. So, although the team had the most outrageous challenge to date, it had the confidence and experience to know that, through sweat and turmoil, it could get the job done.

Strategy Three: Planning the Corporate Approach to Product Development

To go a step futher and provide vision and direction for not only the product but also the company, Close used a Powers of 10 analysis on the company itself and its approach to develop its product. Every company should perform this self-assessment to better understand how its products relate to its corporate mission and brand. So many industrial companies lack any brand statement. Creating a brand statement can be a difficult task for an established company accustomed to a project-based philosophy. But the company's brand statement is critical to its conversion to a process of organic growth. The company's brand can lead the brand directions for the products themselves.

The macro-level analysis of the corporate strategy sets the tone for the culture of the product team, the corporate requirements for a product, the interaction between the company and society at large, and the corporate values and brand attributes. The corporate strategy determines resources for any product and, at a high level, how those resources can be distributed. It sets the direction for partners with other companies in developing and delivering a product or service. The corporate strategy determines the relationship between the company and the local community and the global infrastructure. The corporate strategy must recognize who competitors are and what threats they present, or how the threat of a new technology from the corporation may trigger responses from the competition. Most important is that all of these aspects have a direct impact on the direction and quality of any product developed.

For RedZone, a key component of the corporate strategy is continual innovation. To achieve that goal, it implemented a state-of-the-art product development process to provide a continuing stream of innovations. RedZone began with the innovation process discussed in this book with aspects detailed in *Creating Breakthrough Products*. It then developed a tracking mechanism that followed user research into customer requirements through to engineering specifications. Close believed this to be a necessary step to turn a tech-focused company into a complete-product company.

Another key component of the corporate strategy is to build a corporate identity, a brand. In a business-to-business context, the product is the primary communicant of brand, so product identity and corporate identity are strongly linked. Discussion of color, form language, and logo early in the process connected the product identity to that of RedZone as a company. A mantra of "innovation, not invention" required the company to maintain its expertise in robotics but focus on delivering technology to meet market needs rather than developing the next cutting-edge technical capability only because it could. The product, then, needed to communicate innovation, technical expertise, and the importance of the user, because these were core to the company's identity.

Why would the company care about a color scheme for a robot that will sit inside a sewer? Because the robot spends a good amount of its time outside the pipes, where people see and interact with it. At industry trade shows the robot will stand out against the competition to clearly communicate that "there is something different here."

The realization of the need to communicate corporate identity via the product as well as product identity, and the realization that how people interact with the product will make or break the intended paradigm shift, led Close to hire an industrial designer as one of the first employees of his newly invigorated company. Close charged him to develop a color scheme for the product, an ergonomic interface, and the communication and visualization of all the ongoing stakeholder research that the team participates in. Because this product would establish the company's brand, it was critical to adopt a look and color scheme that would protect the product from competitive reaction. The market was worldwide, and existing U.S. companies tended to make their products look like *Star Wars* spacecrafts, a look that Europeans did not appreciate. So the product was given a clean, simple geometric look that appealed to both U.S. and European buyers, a decision to help both product sales and the company's image.

The Result: Sewer Repair and Beyond

The result is an industrial product that works in extreme environments. The product, called the Renovator, functions off a sled platform with cylindrical components that fits into pipes. The functional need of the product's environment—pipes—produced a natural visual theme. The cylindrical features create continuity in the visual aesthetic. Cylindrical skids on the bottom of the robot curve upward, forming ergonomic handles that make carrying and deploying the robot easy to do. The robat's weight, distribution, and overall dimensions are specified to enable easy manipulation by the crew. Even the camera has a circular theme, with its spherical shape and circular lens openings. Because the platform will house multiple tools, and because quick swap-in/swap-out components are used to make maintenance and repair rapid and on-site, all handles are color-coded for high visibility and are textured to maintain grip in slippery conditions. The name RedZone was extended into the product aesthetics by using red anodized components as highlights on a basic aluminum finish with black details. This theme was also extended to the printed material. For safety, sensors connected to indicator lights positioned on the robot and attachments warn users before tools are activated. The functional capabilities and device aesthetic create a brand language for the product and company.

The stakeholder analysis, the corporate strategy, and the product strategy are integrated with each other. For example, if the crew is enthusiastic in using the robot and becomes more effective in their job, the general contractor (like Sal) who initially is testing the new approach will have positive reinforcement, causing him to purchase additional equipment. RedZone's brand equity will increase, and the products success will reinforce the development team and its process. Their renewed energy will continue to produce successful products that meet the customer's needs. Society as a whole will have a positive response as their tax dollars are more effectively spent and their lives have less disruption, with their yards no longer being dug up. Environmental groups will be positive about improved sewage and less leakage into the water stream. They will petition for new policies that set RedZone's approach as the standard, reinforcing the company's brand and profitability.

We worked with Close in developing this strategic plan. It became clear that this robot was not just a product. It was the future of RedZone. This robot would establish the company and its brand, and the initial product release would set up all the company's subsequent products in the industry. As we write this book, RedZone is involved in its launch of this product. Initial customer reaction has been strong. The upfront strategic planning exercise and extensive research on its stakeholder base has expanded the company's vision of its product platform. If it succeeds, it will corner the market. RedZone will have opened doors for new products with different functions—not only for lateral cutting, but for all the major steps in sewer and water-pipe rehabilitation. Eric Close has the vision and courage to go for this biggest prize, to use this product to define the company and its brand. You never get a second chance to make a first impression, to define fantasy for an industry.

Like those highlighted in Chapter 1, "The New Breed of Innovator," and throughout this book, Eric Close is a new breed of innovator. To him, innovation is "the ability to enter a marketplace, anticipate the needs of the consumer, and put together a product or service that makes their life better." He is a technical guy who loves products. Complete products. His approach is to take successful product development methods from the commercial and retail sectors and apply them to the industrial sector. The innovation process outlined in Chapter 9, "A Process for Product Innovation," does just that. It helps people move away from individual solutions to team-based results. It helps teams communicate with each other and with their customers to understand the requirements and demands from the market. It provides an approach for the team to weigh the conflicts between different stakeholders' needs. By putting together a team that complements each other, and by developing a culture that relishes creativity, Close can build a company along with a product.

Close sees himself as a pragmatist. He embraces design and implements the innovation process we have described because "it works!" and a company in any field "must have it." In the industrial frontier, this leads to a differentiated business model, one that allows his companies to stand out from and lead the pack.

RedZone Robotics is just one example of an industrial-based product company that embraces the mantra that form and function fulfill fantasy. The form and function together stand out in terms of performance and comfort to the user, providing not only a great experience, but also a fantasy projection of a more amenable work environment. For a crew working in the sewer, the form and function of the sewer robot fulfills fantasy. Rather than work deep inside the sewers, the crew can stay clean inside a comfortable cabin, controlling this high-tech robot with the same skill and enthusiasm they had with video games as they grew up.

The World Above the Sewer

From sewer robots to respirators to machine tools to agricultural equipment, innovative companies understand that if they don't embrace user-based design as a means to profit, others will. We are seeing a renaissance in how the industrial frontier is envisioned. As with the first Raymond Loewy-designed Sears Coldspot refrigerator, which in 1935 transformed the refrigerator from a utility machine that stayed on the back porch into a lifestyle device that became an interior feature of every home, the industrial frontier is being transformed into a lifestyle environment where people spend the significant part of their day. Good design is often found and highlighted in the consumer world. But design to create fantasy—yes, even fantasy—has a place in every world where humans interact with their environment, including the world of B-to-B.

When Eric Close took over RedZone, it had a reputation for invention but not for pragmatic innovation. Close could have gone completely the other way to become a component supplier of robotic core technology for other companies. Close realized this was not a sustainable option, instead seeking an opportunity to develop and manufacture a core product with a long-term strategic plan. Close sees the potential of RedZone as a company to branch out and find new applications for its unique robotic design capability.

In Hong Kong, companies are forming a new strategy supported by local government and industry. They have described it as moving from supplier to designer to strategist. Many companies in Hong Kong have been service companies for large global corporations or have found a niche in low-end consumer markets. They realize their future lies in moving from a mind-set of supplier to product designer and producer and, eventually, to industry strategist, setting the future of product development. Hong Kong wants to become the gateway to the Pearl River Delta on the mainland and to help existing and emerging Chinese companies make this same strategic shift.

Suppliers are primarily cost-driven and directed heavily by external companies that purchase their products and services. Original product designers and manufacturers move to develop their own products that, although they often meet current demand, may not be trend-setting. Japanese and Korean companies went through the phase of product design and producer, but now they are at the strategist level. Toyota used to make cheap cars that undersold U.S. and European competition; now it leads the world as a strategic design-driven company that is arguably the most successful car company in the world. In Korea, Lucky Gold Star used to be a supplier making inexpensive components for the computer industry. It then broke out to design and manufacture its own computers, but still it competed by price. It became an industry strategist when it shifted to LG and started to produce world-class electronic equipment. Samsung and Hyundai followed the same path. If your company is built around a supplier mind-set, you must start the process of shifting from supplier to product designer and manufacturer on the way to industry strategist. If you don't want to fight the low-margin battle to be the lowest-cost provider, you simply have no other choice.

8

MAKING DECISIONS FOR PROFIT—SUCCESS EMERGING FROM CHAOS

Innovation is not just about a good idea; it is a process of managing what can appear to be an army of people over a set amount of time making multiple interconnected decisions. Rather than micromanaging, let the product requirements guide the legions who make the detailed daily trade-offs. Yes, these product requirements emerge from an early research and planning stage that is chaotic. But that is good— for the chaos enables exploration and learning. The more you can learn about your market, the better the framework for your decisions.

Toronto, Canada. Jimmie Spear needed a new truck. His Silverado had lasted eight years, and it was costing him as much to maintain it as his car payments used to cost. His truck was his life, or at least his livelihood. Jimmie worked on independent construction. He worked on somewhat sophisticated construction jobs, building additions and the like. But he mostly worked independently, usually hiring a high-school kid to help him out. He liked the freedom. In the eight years since he bought his truck, lots had changed in his life. He was now married with two kids. His weekends and even some nights were filled with family things, from food shopping to going to the park with the kids and the dog. So his wife was on his case to rethink his truck purchase. She wanted a family car, one that could safely drive the kids around. Jimmie needed a workhorse, but it was more. His truck was him. It was a statement of who he is! He wanted a truck with meat, one that looked like it could handle the tough jobs he gave it. He knew he was pretty hard on the vehicle. Some trucks looked wimpy. They probably were.

Jimmie decided to take the kids out Saturday to look around. He visited GM first and was intrigued by the Chevy Avalanche, which had a rear seat that folded down to increase the truck bed size. It looked great. It could be a two-row family vehicle on weekends and his construction truck on weekdays. He then found the Nissan Titan with its four doors, its full truck bed, and the ability to fold up the rear seats for extra storage space for his tools when the kids were not around. Nissans were hot! The strong front with the extensive use of chrome not only looked great but gave him the reassurance that the truck was made of solid parts. Although the kids had had enough and really wanted to just go home and watch TV, he also stopped by the Ford dealer. The new F-150 was inviting. The truck sure looked tough on the outside, but, if he really wanted to splurge, he could get that cushy leather interior.

It used to be that a truck was a truck was a truck. What amazed Jimmie was the amount of choice he had and the amount of feature comfort he could enjoy in a truck. He could justify the tough-looking exterior with safety and comfort for his family. Who would've thought that, with the goal of dragging around a 4×8 sheet of plywood and some tools, there could be this much variation in trucks?

Complexity in the Decision-Making Process

Think about the amount of work it takes to design a toothbrush. There are only two main parts: the handle and the bristles. But the handle may be a bit intricate, with an area that flexes and co-molded rubber on the plastic so that there is a solid grip when the brush is wet. The bristles are of different lengths and angles. Some clean around the gum line, others flex to clean between the teeth, and still others brush the tooth surface. Deciding on each of these toothbrush features takes significant research and decision making. This includes a thorough understanding of the mouth and teeth, material analysis of flex performance and oral compatibility, and a thorough understanding of the ergonomics and physiology of the hand and arm.

To ensure that the intended market finds the product appealing, the product team must be aware of trends in the bathroom and kitchen and of general fashion trends in colors and shapes. The team must know the latest materials that are available and might potentially be used in the product and the latest manufacturing techniques that might allow for the next innovation. A toothbrush must be sold in a package at the point of purchase that stands out and sells the toothbrush inside, and variations of packaging must be designed and prototyped for market tests, with those tests conducted and analyzed well before the product launch. The package must also connect to the lifestyle of the person who is buying it.

There are also legal issues. In the case of intellectual property, you need to make sure you are not infringing on another's patents and, if not, are protecting your unique idea with both design and utility patents to limit potential of rip-offs. Also, a product that is put inside a person's mouth carries liability issues. The label on the package has to have every important piece of legal information required by whatever federal agency is responsible for protecting the public from poorly designed, dangerous toothbrushes and from product misuse. If a problem arises from poor information or product misuse, the other side of the corporate legal department will be called into action. Not only is product liability a nightmare for a particular product team, it also can have an impact on the company brand identity.

Next time you are in your local drugstore, look at the number of toothbrushes you have to choose from. It was not long ago that a simple bend in the handle under the product name Reach was seen as a big breakthrough, but in product development terms, that design was a century ago.

As noted, a typical toothbrush has two parts. Now let's bring it up a notch and think about the innovation breakthrough for the next toaster. A toaster has 20 parts and it is an electric appliance. You have significantly upped the product's complexity and the number of decisions that must be made.

If you are designing a new car, you take the complexity up further by a power of 1,000, to 20,000 parts. Every part must be designed or specified, and many of the parts must work in unison as a subsystem. Subsystems must then work in concert to meet the vehicle's performance requirements. Often, to achieve the best performance in one subsystem, another must work below expectations. For instance, the addition of a small oil pump can dramatically extend engine life. The trade-off is that this oil pump would circulate the oil immediately before a cold engine start, so the benefit of this pump would cost multiple seconds of delay before the car could start. Thus, trade-offs are considered and aspects of the product redesigned until the overall product is satisfactory. The best vehicles perform beyond expectation and deliver an optimal experience that surprises and delights the customer. Given that the vehicle's product development cycle is still about three years or more, consider the vast number of decisions that must be made and that effectively come together to produce a successful (or unsuccessful) vehicle. How many of those decisions can be wrong and still produce an affordable, appealing, and profitable car or truck?

When you are driving your car, with its 20,000 parts, imagine the number of things that have to go right. Hundreds of people have to be coordinated over several years in a cohesive plan. Innovation is not just about a good idea; it is a process of managing what can at times appear to be an army of people over a set amount of time making multiple interconnected decisions. For example, as an initial concept establishes a product direction, a brand statement must be developed, including marketing insights, visual strategy, and an attribute strategy. At the same time, there is a need to establish technical constraints such as standards and manufacturing capabilities. There are also technical development issues and the development of a market model. Further down the process, there are financial issues in allocating budgets and determining the product's feature content from all the options that are considered. There is the customer strategy that includes feature packages offered in different models of the product. There are decisions on acceptable and anticipated levels of manufacturing quality and expectations on the product's fit and finish (otherwise known as *craftsmanship*) and the technical feasibility and reliability of the technologies and manufacturing methods. In every successful product, many key decisions must be made if the potential innovation will reach maximum potential and generate the equity in brand and profit needed to sustain a company.

Organizing the Decision-Making Process

Not only are there numerous decisions, but each decision is related to many others, typically as a trade-off. There is no way to make a product, say an SUV, that has high fuel efficiency, lots of cargo room, three rows of seats, premium features, high performance, tight crafts-manship, and individualized feature choices, all at a low cost. Choices are made, and aspects are sacrificed. Some vehicles are exciting to drive and have all the comforts of your living room and cost more than many homes, while others are barely tolerable to sit in but can carry a load and are affordable to a large market. The former vehicle likely has a high price and high margins with low volumes, while the latter has a lower price and lower margins but high sales volume.

There are different approaches to managing the trade-offs. The commodity or cost-focused company sees the decision process as one to design a product for mass consumption at minimal cost, so financial considerations serve as arbiters of ideas. As the product's unique and most beneficial aspects are compromised for cost considerations, eventual margins also narrow. The narrow margins lead again to the need for additional cost cutting. The resulting product tends to sit in a competitive space with low price and low margins.

The high value-differentiation lifestyle-oriented company sees differentiation as the ultimate goal, to achieve a new level of experi-ence for the customer. The lifestyle-driven approach promotes aes-thetics and usability as the driver, with technical superiority fulfilling performance expectations. The result may be lower levels of produc-tion but at much higher margins.

The pragmatic innovation company balances these two extremes with a product that supports its brand, stands out in the crowd, and is priced to reach an appropriate market. Its customer-focused approach understands cost limitations based on an expectation of per-formance and features in consideration of the context of use of the product. In other words, the customer-focused approach delivers a high value differentiation within the purchaser's financial means.

If cost were the ultimate arbiter of trade-offs, decisions would be fairly straightforward. Whichever option would be cheapest overall would win out. But because virtually no company uses costs as the only criterion, at least successfully, how do innovative companies manage the host of decisions?

The StageGate model of product development is one good baseline for companies to use and many do. StageGate defines deliverables across the product development process that must be met to move through one "gate" to the next stage in the process.[1] The five stages are major project activities run sequentially from scoping out a market to launching a product, while the gates are checklists to make sure each stage was sufficiently explored. Although the foundation is appropriate, the problem is that all the models companies generate in using this and similar approaches are ideals. These ideal models are often generated by committee, appointed by management, and given to teams without their understanding why the model was developed and adopted, or even the motivation behind the steps. The teams never interpret the model for their application. No product program actually runs like the ideal model. When a team reaches a roadblock or has to deal with input that was not anticipated, it often falls behind and may never figure out how to adapt to the change. The models don't tell the team *how* to meet the gate requirements, especially the early ones critical for innovation, just what they are.

Managing product development using a pragmatic, innovative approach is a challenge. It requires balancing equal and opposite forces. The best managers seem to find a way to keep the big picture and goal in mind and also feel free to vary the program as it develops. Instead of hoping the program will go according to the ideal, these managers realize from the beginning that the ideal is there as reference for support, not a process carved in stone. They can shift and interpret the process as needed and address new issues that arise as the inevitable variation happens, adjusting accordingly. Instead of feeling threatened and trying to make the ideal process model fit the unanticipated issue, they enjoy the sport of meeting challenges.

---

1   Cooper, R. G. *Winning at New Products: Accelerating the Process from Idea to Launch.* Perseus Publishing, Cambridge, 2001.

We use the concept of rock climbing to help you understand this approach. You can plan a climb and set your path, but even if you have climbed a mountain before, every climb is a new experience. Weather can vary and change the conditions. Your approach will vary no matter how much you may want to keep it the same. The mountain itself can change, making terrain more or less easy to navigate. Aron Ralston became famous for his incredible, almost superhuman ability to overcome defeat when he was stranded while rock climbing in the wilderness alone. A large boulder fell and pinned his arm. He had to make a life-altering decision. Ralston calmly realized that the only thing to do was to cut off his arm; otherwise, he would surely die. Not only did he effectively do that (we will let you read the details elsewhere on your own), recognizing that he had to apply a tourniquet or he would bleed to death, he then had to climb down the mountain face, lowering himself down a sheer cliff with only one arm, and walk an extensive distance to find help. His actions are a testament to what a person can do to survive. He sees himself as a stronger person for the experience and has turned a disaster into a personal triumph. He is the epitome of grace under pressure. He found the resources internally to survive the unpredictable obstacle. Because he was a good planner, he knew how to adjust the plan rather than sit there helplessly and starve to death. He has written a book, *Between a Rock and a Hard Place*,[2] and has appeared on numerous TV shows. Just when you think you are at the brink of disaster, it is always possible to find the opportunity to turn impending doom into an unprecedented success if you can just step back and see the big picture. You need a process that gives you structure, and you need to adapt to the unpredictable. This is the foundation of innovation.

2   Ralston, A. *Between a Rock and a Hard Place*. Atria Publishing, 2004.

The Butterfly Effect

Within that structure, if the product development process at times seems chaotic, it is! If a butterfly flaps its wings in Brazil, this could cause a storm in Belgium the next week. You have heard the story or maybe have seen the movie. This is the basis of the mathematics of chaos, where a small event can have enormous and unpredictable consequences down the road. The decision-making process in product development has many similarities to the butterfly flapping its wings, the seemingly small event. Decision making, like wing flapping, is highly causal: one apparently insignificant decision can significantly affect the outcome, just like one flap of the butterfly's wings can have a profound effect on the weather.

So it is with product development that every decision affects every other decision, with one decision connected to the next, and each downstream decision dependent on previous choices. If a slightly different decision were made—say, to create a different visual line in a vehicle, or select a different spring mechanism in a toaster, or choose a different material for the bristles in a toothbrush—the implications of those decisions produce a very different vehicle, toaster, or toothbrush.

Unlike the butterfly, product developers can influence the outcome of the process. The research, insight, and feel for the product and process allow them to make decisions that are likely to lead to more successful outcomes. Each informed or insightful decision affects the next informed or insightful decision, and so on. The butterfly wing flapping is very much a random occurrence in the weather system; the butterfly at best can control its own flight and has no awareness beyond its own activities. The butterfly does not understand causation. Successful product developers understand the cause-effect relationship and the overall implications of feature selection and form choices for the product's gestalt—how the product looks and functions as a whole. Unfortunately, some product

developers are more like the butterfly. They make independent decisions without a thorough understanding of the market opportunity,
the customer, or the rest of the product as a whole, never understanding why their product falters or fails in the marketplace.

The butterfly flapping its wings is, for the weather system, a random event. Decision making in product development is not. That
said, many random influences provide fodder for decision making.
For example, the brainstorming process used so frequently early in
design to stimulate ways of conceptualizing possible product solutions is wrought with random thoughts and analogies. The seemingly
random thought process is filtered with an early understanding of the
marketplace, directing the process toward a blissful instead of stormy
end.

Throughout the product development process, random external
events do occur that cannot be predicted. Political and social events
rapidly change needs and desires of a customer base. Increased gas
prices lead to concern about gas mileage and, eventually, fewer trucks
and SUVs sold. As a result of 9/11, there is less travel and more focus
on safety. It is hard to predict what the competition will do. A dis-
ruptive technology, or even one that makes small but noticeable
improvements, may mean disruption in bringing a product to market.

Some of these external events are devastating to a product or
company, whereas others are not. As a result of 9/11, most airlines in
the United States struggled while respirator company Mine Safety
Appliance had record earnings as people purchased gas masks in
record numbers. Although an event like 9/11 was unexpected, and its
impact on the economy and psyche clearly was unusual, it does illustrate the need for a system that is robust to random influences. New
Balance, having made the social decision to keep a portion of its
products "made in America," was positioned to stand against foreign
competition and American competitors that made their products
overseas as people in the United States made emotion-based
purchases after 9/11.

Chaos Within Structure

Although the external influences are unpredictable, a structure to good product development guides the process to success and provides methods to improve the robustness of decision making. The structure of the product development process guides you through the unknown, helping you define your goals, constraints, and variables. Every product opportunity has a different set of goals (what you want to achieve), constraints (things you cannot change), and variables (things you can and must change). The challenge in developing truly innovative products is first to identify a unique set of goals, then to identify a set of variables that can be modified to reach those goals, and then to understand the real versus perceived constraints on those variables.

When Palm Computing came out with its first PDA, its competitors believed the form factor to be a real constraint, because the computing power (and the larger chips back then) required to recognize handwriting took up substantial space. Palm's innovative solution came from the recognition that form factor was a variable after all, at least as long as customers were willing to learn a new graffiti alphabet. Palm's innovation launched the whole PDA category, which had thus far been a flop. The butterfly flaps its wings within the constraints of physics. The product development process must work within the bounds of physics, but it is also influenced by humans, culture, society, and thought, all of which were key to Palm's success.

The structure of the process does not define the goals, constraints or variables—it does not do the work for you. It provides guidance on how to navigate the space of the unknown. It helps you make robust decisions based on insights and incomplete or even incorrect facts. The fodder it provides to make those decisions is based on the centrality of the customer. The customer unites all divisions of the innovative company—the user is the fulcrum that balances goals, constraints, and variables.

The fuzzy front end, or the early stage of product innovation, will be chaotic. That chaos is a good thing. It enables exploration and learning. The more you can learn about your market, the better your filter on the chaotic ideation process. Chaos helps with the accuracy in finding and defining a good product direction. Later, the process begins to change. There is enough focus, enough variables and constraints identified, that the system begins to be more predictable, that precision becomes the focus. Although not every random event downstream can be anticipated, many can, and a robust process thinks about scenarios of disruption. Some can be designed for, making a robust product with longevity in the market; others cannot. Accepting chaos allows you to more aptly deal with random impact as it takes place, to work with it rather than against it. Rather than fight it, be the choreographer of the chaos.

If you squash the chaos, you squash the exploration and research so critical to the success of developing a product. You work hard to produce a quality manufactured product. You later find out that your precision was on but your accuracy was off, that the market does not want your well-made product because it does not meet their expectations of the product's experience of use or purpose. You find yourself scrambling to add or remove features, not understanding that their inherent interconnectedness causes functional, aesthetic, or manufacturing problems with other features. Your soft and hard quality goes down, and you scramble to make both satisfactory.

Interdisciplinary Decision Making

All exploration centers around the customer, at least tangentially if not directly. Marketers are well acquainted with customer research, as are industrial designers. But the technology and financial people should connect with the customer as well. We have found that the best companies have integrated teams that engage in customer research together. Different disciplines are trained to interpret information in a different way, so the integrated and inclusive team is more likely to have a richer understanding of customer needs and desires, and thus a better understanding of priorities as the design process proceeds.

To see the value of integrated teams, consider the opposite case, the extreme case of dominance by single viewpoints. The technology company tends to emphasize the product's performance, technology capabilities, and manufacturing capabilities. These high-tech products are technically state-of-the-art but often miss the boat on customer satisfaction. These companies excel at quality programs with precise results but miss the accuracy of the market and lack true innovation. Many technology companies provide business-to-business products or services and have seduced themselves with the notion that they do not need to worry about nontechnology product features. However, these companies are vulnerable to competitors that can provide products with hard and soft quality.

Cost-oriented companies emphasize financial and resource allocation decisions. The result is often an unexciting but predictable product with slim margins. These products often find themselves considered or competing with commodities. Rumor has it that the canned soups on today's shelves taste nothing like the same products of yesteryear, that manufacturers have little by little switched to cheaper ingredients. Such is the way of cost-oriented companies in mature product categories.

Marketing-oriented firms emphasize price promotions, direct-mail flyers, and highly touted but trivial updates to their product lines. Lemon-scented, anyone? Style-oriented companies emphasize decisions based on aesthetics and trends. These products are exciting to look at and trendy to own but often are impractical for long-term use, or at times even short-term use.

Each discipline has something to bring to the table, essential viewpoints and skills for competitive firms. Each needs to understand the customer so that they can set the macro structure in place, so that trade-offs do not compromise what the product is planned to offer, so that the product is not brought to a market that expects another. Pragmatic innovators solve this dilemma by understanding the customer through extensive research, setting decision priorities based on that understanding, and maintaining that priority throughout the product development process.

To consider why integrated decisions are needed in practice, consider one experience of an automobile firm as it was in the midst of a grille redesign. Grilles are one feature of a vehicle that makes a statement about the vehicle's personality. In people's minds, this translates to the ability for those who drive the vehicle to make a statement about who they are, or at least who they want to be. Grilles can be large and bold, with strong, thick, vertical lines, as with a Hummer; they can be refined and simple, with horizontal stripes, as with a Cadillac; or they can be subtle and nondescript, as found in many Pontiacs. Hummer, Cadillac, and Pontiac are all brands of GM, but each makes a unique brand and aesthetic statement, partially through various grille designs. The Buick brand, for example, has a unique grille only when it has an oval base with a small bump in the middle on top. Remove that bump, and the grille looks a lot like a Ford oval. The grille is a critical aesthetic feature that defines a vehicle's brand identity and personality. In the case of Jimmie Spear that began this chapter, one of the biggest factors in the impression of the strength of a pickup truck is the grille. The Avalanche, Titan, and F-150 all suggest a different personality partly because of their grilles.

In the production of vehicles, every year car companies modify vehicle features or aesthetic ornamentation to freshen up the look. About every seven years a major redesign, possibly down to the level of the platform itself, is taken on. The fixed investment for tooling of the vehicles is so expensive that large portions have to be reused each year to pay back those costs, until the major redesign occurs. Even in those major redesign years, there is usually some level of carryover; in other words, some of the parts are reused—"carried over" from the previous design.

We observed the redesign process of a vehicle during the overhaul year at one auto company. The grille became an issue of note. To save costs, the grille was originally slated as a carryover part, one that was used on the previous model vehicle. It looked great there, so why not use it again? Although this company was effective at producing successful vehicles, there was a lapse in focus on and shared understanding of the customer. The finance groups drove the decision-making process for the vehicle's early direction. The vehicle sold well, but the economy was shifting, so excess spending was carefully watched. The initial program description called for the carryover grille.

Over time, however, the design studio argued that the grille needed to be redesigned to support the vehicle's new emerging image and style. They argued for a significant increase in budget and time to incorporate that change. At the same time, engineering, with a lack of understanding of the integrity of aesthetic features, argued to keep the carryover part to meet the cost and timing targets given to them by finance. This stemmed from a finance group that refused to allocate resources to modify that part. The studio eventually won the argument, and the grille was redesigned. If the project management team had better done their homework on the customer upfront, they would have included the voice of the studio before the program description was set. Their priorities would have been different. Instead, the program was delayed and the cost target missed because of this design conflict. The company was pragmatic enough to recognize its error before it was too late. The production vehicle not only has a unique and strong brand identity, with a bold grille at its forefront, but the vehicle has been a major success in the marketplace.

To understand why so many companies default to a commodity mentality in decision making, which was really the problem in the grille conflict, consider again the vast number of decisions that have to be made throughout the process. There are many variables in the product being designed. A car has upward of 20,000 parts. Each part has several features that must be identified, modeled, and designed through variables. Many of these variables are interconnected in that deciding the solution to one affects the solution of others; the variables are constrained to influence each other. Physical, aesthetic, legal, and financial constraints limit the realization of the variables. It is understandable that technologists focus on those variables that they can understand and model, and the same goes for finance and even design. It takes effort and insight to work as a team in communicating and negotiating solutions for all of these variables.

The interconnectedness of the variables is often quite tight. A slight change in one variable may profoundly affect how other variables are chosen as the process proceeds. That is the effect of chaos, which is so often squashed too soon. If the team at the auto company decided to carry over the grille, the influence on the car's aesthetic is much different than if the grille is redesigned. The same is true about the features of the grille as it is redesigned. If it is bold, the vehicle takes a bold stand, and all the other aesthetic details must align with its look and feel.

To not have costs end up as the ultimate arbiter of decisions, it is important to account for the perspectives of the different functional areas that relate to the product, to rely on a research and development process that integrates the viewpoints of performance engineers, industrial or studio designers, marketers, finance, manufacturing, technology development, and customer research. All this input is needed because variables are understood by and often controlled by each of these disciplines. These perspectives blend together for decision making to achieve a solution that maximizes the potential for each within the context of the others. Within the structured research and design process that crosses functions, the at-times chaotic countless daily decisions about variables can be effectively managed. To use the drinking-from-a-fire-hose analogy, the cross-functional product design process is the hose that can be pointed in various strategic directions, while the day-to-day decisions are allowed to pour through, uncontrolled at first.

Finally, a certain amount of chaos exists and has to occur in the system. If you allow it to flourish early, if it is channeled well, it becomes a benefit, because it allows greater exploration in the early process. Rather than getting bogged down in analyzing every last decision early, let the customer insight lead you to your next decision point; let the process guide you.

9

A PROCESS FOR
PRODUCT INNOVATION

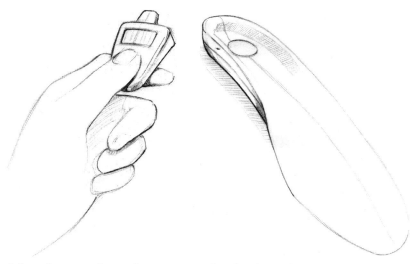

Although preceding chapters in this book each contain their own examples of people, products, companies, and issues, each chapter's illustrations focus on specific topics—the individual oaks, hickories, pines, and dogwoods of the forest. This chapter provides an overview of the innovation forest itself using an example from an R&D relationship between a university and the athletic apparel company New Balance. We describe a process for structuring the early "fuzzy front end" of product development from opportunity to product approval, showing how innovators implement the process and tools we describe in earlier chapters.

Sedona, AZ. "This really is God's country," thought Karen Anderson, her feet pounding the red packed trails, as Bono sang the words on her iPod. U2 had probably never even visited Sedona. The red rocks jutted out into large cathedral peaks. The trees sent out a rich evergreen scent. And the air was dry and clean and hot!

Next week was the race, and this was Karen's weekly Saturday trip from Phoenix out to Sedona to train. On-site training gave her an extra thrill; that alone was worth the two-hour drive. Plus, she could indulge in her ritual post-training recovery stop for an energy-enhanced cherry papaya smoothie.

Karen remembered running as a kid. She had started running in middle school, on Cocopah's cross-country team. Practices were early morning, before school. She remembered how she often felt shaky after runs, after pounding the roads. She wondered whether the early runs were to blame for her poor concentration in her first class of the day, history. She had always needed recovery time, time to sit and drink a smoothie, although smoothies did not exist back then.

How things had changed. The Phoenix area was nothing like what it was in 1965, the year her school had opened. Back then, for instance, Cocopah Middle School was the northern outpost of the Scottsdale school district, located next to Camelback Mountain in Paradise Valley. Now, when Karen's kids are attending Cocopah, it is the geographic center of the school district.

Not only was life changing, but products were, too. Karen's new running shoes, for instance, were great. The guy at the New Balance store was right. Karen wondered how a company can make changes—and, in this case, improvements—to a product again and again. She always bought New Balance running shoes. She had tried others, but there really was none better.

The consistent ankle support and the improved cushioning seemed to relieve the pain as she ran. At the age of 44, she had thought her running days were over, but her switch to New Balance gave her running career new life. She enjoyed weekend 10Ks, and she enjoyed escaping from the routine of her week. She realized that for all the wear and effort she put her body through, it was, really, the shoes that allowed her to keep going.

New Balance

New Balance is a midsized company out of Boston, a privately held player in an intensely competitive market. The company began by producing arch supports in 1906. It evolved into a niche company that produced running shoes for the serious athlete. The low-volume market kept the company focused and lean, with early manufacturing primarily in New England. As its reputation spread, that its shoes were the choice of serious runners, so did the demand for its product. Amateur weekend athletes like Karen started choosing New Balance, and soon an almost cult-like following evolved.

Today, New Balance focuses on running and court shoes with a theme of fit and comfort. They are known for quality. Some of the shoes are made in the United States, separating them from Nikes which not only are made offshore but also have run into social problems after reports that they are made in sweatshops in Asia. After 9/11, New Balance did not suffer the same decline in sales as other manufacturers, partly due to its "made in the USA" policy. Although only about 20 percent of its shoes are still made in the United States, this still stands out as a local commitment in a time where tight margins keep prices low and competitive. Further, the globalization of manufacturing is no longer just an economic consideration. Asian technologies have, in many instances, surpassed U.S. capabilities. So competitors at times go to Asia, not only for cost but also manufacturing quality. Keeping shoes "made in the USA" holds brand equity, which overcomes economic costs.

Customers are loyal to the brand. "Comfort and fit" drives the product and is the New Balance identity. Manufacturing quality is consistently high. New Balance advertises but has no high-profile Michael, Tiger, or Kobe endorsements. It is a privately owned company that does not feel compelled to compete with the approaches used by its competitors. In the markets where word of mouth is a strong alternative to paid advertising, New Balance excels; however, in the markets where names as icons have sway in schoolyards and playing fields, its position is not as competitive. The company has been willing to accept that compromise, and in many ways, this has added to its sense of integrity as the shoe company for serious runners. Interestingly enough, this perceived value has spilled over into the nonrunning shoe market, where, certain high-school students whose gear for everyday life includes backpacks and Nalgene plastic bottles for drinking water have extended that trend and designated New Balance as the casual shoe of choice.

New Balance products nicely balance cutting-edge technology, especially in material use, ergonomics of fit, and appropriate but reserved aesthetic trends. Although New Balance meets the industry standard of new product introduction four or more times a year, it shies away from high-fashion trends and instead improves each product line. Its shoes are named by number, with increasing numeric value generally meaning a higher-performance and higher-priced shoe.

Innovation by Cooperation

As companies struggle to find new competitive advantage, they are using a number of techniques to stimulate organic growth. These approaches include working with respected experts to run workshops and hiring consulting firms to support and bring new perspectives. To extend R&D capability, some companies turn to universities to conduct research and exploration into areas the company does not otherwise have time or resources to explore. New Balance has an advanced product group, led by Edith Harmon, who we discussed in Chapter 1, "The New Breed of Innovator," which is the greenhouse for organic growth in the company.

Harmon approached Carnegie Mellon University because she believes that the outcome of such relationships can complement and stimulate organic growth internally. She wanted the university to use its course in Integrated Product Development to explore new opportunities for New Balance. She wanted to see what integrated teams of students could achieve with direction from faculty and her New Balance group, for their performance would illustrate what could be achieved with similar teams in-house.

The award-winning course at Carnegie Mellon integrates teams of students in industrial design, engineering, and marketing, supported by four faculty advisors representing three different colleges in the university. This course has a history of successful product concepts, demonstrating the power of the innovation process. There are now examples of other universities evolving a similar cooperative product development approach, a trend for companies to take advantage of.

The Carnegie Mellon course with New Balance yielded six successful product concepts for New Balance through six student teams in 16 weeks. This chapter focuses on one of those product concepts. The success of the course demonstrates the payoff of the innovation process, and it helped New Balance recognize how it could develop products internally that it had been outsourcing. Over the years, the course has helped convince individuals such as Dee Kapur and Edith Harmon and companies such as Ford and New Balance that the innovation process delivers a high rate of return on investment.

A Case Study in Innovation for New Balance: Four Phases of New Product Development

This chapter illustrates a comprehensive methodology that includes the issues and tools presented in earlier chapters. It begins with how companies identify opportunities to develop new products, how they expand their understanding of those opportunities, and how they translate that understanding into a set of product requirements or specifications that fulfill the market's needs. The examples then show how that early set of product requirements leads to a process of product conceptualization and refinement, and eventually production of a product with features tailored to the needs of the individuals in the target market.[1]

For this project, New Balance assigned the team the task of developing a new market opportunity for the growing consumer segment of people who are overweight—not traditionally a market that is targeted by athletic apparel companies. The strategic area was general in nature, not restricted to shoes or clothing or to specific genders or age groups.

Here is a quick overview of the approach. Several factors contribute to the development of new product opportunities. These factors are social, economic, and technological (SET). As these factors change over time, they generate gaps in the marketplace between products and services that exist and the potential for those that would better fulfill market needs, wants, and desires. These gaps, then, create new product and service opportunities. To respond to these opportunities, you need to understand the value that customers will expect in the new product. The customer's expectations of value must

---

1   If you practice product development and want more information, the tools and theory of this process are detailed in Cagan, J. and C. M. Vogel. *Creating Breakthrough Products: Innovation from Product Planning to Program Approval*. Financial Times Prentice Hall, Upper Saddle River, NJ, 2002.

then be translated into product attributes. So understanding the changing social, economic, and technological factors leads to finding opportunities that must then be translated in value and converted into product attributes. It sounds simple when stated this way, but companies struggle, particularly when analyzing customer value expectations. If you do not get the value right, the product will not be successful, no matter how strong your quality program is or how lean your manufacturing capability.

This innovation process is a complement to the downstream programs of quality manufacture. It is a four-phase process that clarifies the earliest innovation stage, often called the "fuzzy front end" of product development. The four phases are 1) identifying a product opportunity, 2) understanding the product opportunity, 3) conceptualizing the product opportunity, and 4) refining the product opportunity. In 16 weeks, this method can support interdisciplinary teams in identifying product opportunities and turn them into fully developed product proposals and patents.

The student team described here followed the four-phase innovation process to create a complete product concept, ready for patent protection. Provisional patents were then filed to give the company time to assess the concept in the context of its business strategy.[2] In the following sections, we walk through the steps of the innovation process while illustrating the development of the product for the growing overweight market.

Phase I: Identifying Product Opportunities

Bob is approaching 50, and his current health and family genes are telling him he better lose the pounds. There are a lot of guys like Bob.

---

2   Provisional patents, discussed further in the next chapter, give a company a year of protection at a reasonable cost before it needs to invest in the more expensive full patent.

In the first phase of the process, product opportunities are identified, starting with research into trends. By the end of this phase, the development team will have identified gaps in the marketplace where a product or service would improve the well-being of the target market. The goal of Phase 1 is to identify one product opportunity. The opportunity must be stated in broad terms, with a focus on the experience of the opportunity, without any hint of a product description. It would be stated something like "a process and/or device to safely protect a child in a car." Most people automatically want to develop a car seat.

Chapter 4, "Identifying Today's Trends for Tomorrow's Innovations," discussed trends and their implications—in particular, the SET factors that interact in a dynamic way to create product opportunities. For instance, the rising number of overweight people worldwide, but especially in America, yields new opportunities for athletic apparel companies to widen their target beyond the fit and trim, to design products for those needing help with a first step toward activity. As Americans become heavier, the pressures to get thin have increased with current emphasis on diet control. Issues of style in fashion have emphasized women more than men. Insurance companies are beginning to consider obesity a disease that could demand some level of reimbursement. This economic factor did not come into play as the eventual product was developed, but it was important to consider in understanding the overall opportunity.

Trends such as these lead to product opportunity gaps in the marketplace. For example, a more sedentary populace expands the market for equipment used in low-exertion exercise, such as walking. A heavier populace puts more stress on shoes, increasing the need for high-performance materials that can better stand the rigors of heavier people. Insights that identify such trends come from customer-based interviews and interactions as well as secondary literature-based reading and research.

The team went in depth in each direction and brainstormed more than 100 product opportunity gaps in the marketplace. Selecting the best opportunity from a field of 100 requires qualitative research with possible users, coupled with a sense of the profit potential of each. Many could develop into exciting and successful products. Insights from potential customers and experts become the filter that selects the one product opportunity that survives. For instance, the product team was composed of students in their early 20s, but after studying the social, economic, and technological factors, they narrowed their target to middle-aged men. As these students moved forward in their work, the decisions were increasingly made for them by the information they had gathered, not by themselves, because they had to look completely outside themselves to properly serve their focal market.

As examples of the range of product opportunities developed in this phase, the team considered changing the orientation of foot entry into a shoe, an all-inclusive measurement system for fitting shoes, and "sexier" walking equipment for that market. Only after much thought and discussion on numerous ideas did the team settle on the opportunity "to allow overweight 40- to 55-year-old men who have long been sedentary and who have become more aware of their health to overcome physical and mental hurdles on the way to establishing an active, healthy lifestyle."

This phase began with general strategic directions and ended with open opportunities, not with product ideas. This first phase defined the scope of the problem to attack, the opportunity to be explored in later phases, and the questions to be answered.

Phase II: Understanding the Product Opportunity

If Bob could walk 10,000 steps a day, he could get enough exercise to lose weight and get himself in better shape. He is willing but does not want to wear a sign saying "Look at me; I'm walking." How can he get feedback and not have to wear something overt for everyone else to see?

The next step in the process is to gain an in-depth and insightful understanding of the user and purchaser and to identify and understand all the influences and implications of the product to them and to the market at large. The example shows how developers translate customer insights into product requirements, which will then form the criteria for assessing concepts developed in Phase III. Engineers and designers often develop concepts with little frame of reference. Without a clear framework for decision making, teams usually fail to choose the most appropriate options. Establishing of a wide range of criteria for a potential product helps support the parallel development of product visual attributes of lifestyle, ergonomic aspects, and core technology. Teams must develop actionable insights that stem from a clear understanding of the stakeholders and a particular focus on emerging needs of the end customer.

This is the key phase for innovation, and this is where many of the ideas and tools discussed in this book become critical. This phase is focused on qualitative research, an approach at times especially difficult for traditional market researchers and engineers, who are trained in the use and comfort of statistics and numbers. It is here that a proposition of value based on customer needs, wants, and desires creates a framework for product innovation. The challenge is to identify, understand, and articulate the key attributes of value and to turn that value proposition into actionable insights that will eventually be developed into a product. It is here that strategic planning (see Chapter 7) and identifying a market in terms of a scenario rather than a statistic (see Chapters 4, and 6) come together in an analysis of market value.

This analysis of the value must be broken into attributes that product developers can act on to develop so that they can produce products that are highly desired by the end users and purchasers. The analysis of value helps transition product development from qualitative insights to realized product features. So we discuss product value before product attributes.

The idea of value is not to get more features for less money. Instead, value is the connection of a user to a product in a way that augments his lifestyle and makes his activities easier and better. Value is the product's ability to fulfill wishes, to meet expectations of fantasy. The challenge is how a product developer understands the value a customer seeks, and translates that understanding into product characteristics. All the research and analysis we have discussed so far provide that understanding. Now they need to be converted into design attributes that evolve into product attributes.

Value Opportunity

We have developed a framework that both represents attributes of value and provides a mechanism to translate those attributes into product requirements. Value can be broken into seven discrete classes, called *value opportunities*, that capture an initial but complete understanding of what people need, want, and desire in the products and services they use.

- **Emotion**

  The first is emotion, the direct connection to the user experience and fantasy. What fantasy do people expect from use of the product? For overweight men who have become aware of their need for a healthier lifestyle, emotion is critical. Products that make them feel powerful and independent will support their choice to be more active, and products that aid their confidence will encourage them as they strive toward a new lifestyle.

- **Ergonomics**

  Next is ergonomics, the attribute that addresses the physical interaction with a product. How easy and intuitive is the product to use? From an interview of a shoe store manager, overweight men were happy just to find a durable shoe that would fit and would have enough initial cushioning to be comfortable. As expected, many larger individuals had trouble donning and removing shoes.

- **Aesthetics**

  Aesthetics includes not only visual, or form, but all the senses that interact in experiencing a product. Overweight men are accustomed to sacrificing aesthetics to live with shoes that are either comfortable or visually appealing, not both. On one hand, such a finding could support the notion that aesthetics could be ignored. On the other hand, any product that met other needs in addition to scoring high on aesthetics could have significant impact.

- **Identity**

  A product is the physical statement of the brand identity and is central to its success. Every experience with a product affects the identity, and identity sets up the experience. Overweight men, like everyone else, use products to make personal statements and to express self-definition. In the arena of health-enabling products, whether enabling shoes or enabling medical devices, products lack identity and differentiation, so an opportunity exists to bring positive self-expression into this market.

- **Impact**

  Next comes impact—addressing the societal influence connected to and addressed by the product. This includes social relevance to groups and individuals, and environmental considerations. As exercise networks and clubs increasingly become a nexus for social interaction, as obesity increasingly captures U.S.

national attention like smoking did a few years ago, the opportunity for societal impact increases the relevance of obesity-related products.

• **Core technology**

Core technology addresses the functions that enable performance. Is the product state-of-the-art in its ability to perform? To date, exercise technologies have concentrated on the needs of those already exercising, not those who are struggling toward an active lifestyle. In shoes, where the provided cushioning does not vary by shoe but the need for cushioning varies by person, the cushioning and reliability are calibrated for the lighter and fitter. So exercise shoes for the heavyset may benefit from technologies to allow for size-appropriate cushioning and performance.

• **Quality**

Quality addresses not only manufacturing quality but also the expectation of how the product will perform overtime. Although traditionally viewed as manufacturing quality, it also includes the product's fit and finish and its durability. How quickly do shoes wear out when used by those with larger bodies?

Innovation begins with understanding how these aspects of value connect customers to market opportunities. The use of this understanding is a sophisticated process of defining each value attribute for a product opportunity and then refining that definition into attributes that a product or service must incorporate to succeed. As the product development process proceeds, the articulation of those attributes gets refined and eventually becomes the product's form and features. Finding a solution that holistically integrates these attributes can be a difficult process of negotiation that requires an innovative outcome. It is this step-by-step process of exploration and refinement that separates comprehensive innovation from technology-focused invention, and also the innovative from the mundane.

Understanding Customers in the Field

Innovative product developers spend time in the field. They observe, interview, and analyze the actual people who will use their product. At New Balance, Josh Kaplan from the advanced product group flies around the country and goes on runs with different lead users, understanding the nuances that make their running experience great. Designers at Whirlpool go on service calls to understand the context of where their product is used and how to make it better; that even includes VP Chuck Jones. CEO Eric Close and the engineers at RedZone spend days on site observing how the crews interact with their equipment and each other to improve the experience of sewer repair.

The student team spent much time studying potential users and other key stakeholders. They extensively read current research on exercise, and they conducted many interviews of adults who were formerly out of shape but had begun to exercise. They found that exercise does not have to be relegated to a reserved part of the day, but that small bouts of exercise scattered throughout the day, like the walk from the car to the office, can accumulate and become a beneficial, healthy, active routine. They found that lack of time was the number one reason for inactivity, that busy lifestyles left no time for aerobic workouts, that these busy individuals were willing to tackle small goals but refused to commit to large lifestyle changes.

The product team narrowed its focus to men in part because a narrower market segment can be more closely matched with design attributes. But there were additional reasons for the increased focus on men. More middle-aged men are overweight than middle-aged women—with 43.25 percent compared to 27.3 percent. Also, men tend to exercise to lose weight, whereas women tend to diet. Finally, New Balance serves a larger proportion of adult men than women, so a focus on men fits well with current company strengths. Men who had stopped exercising may have previously been the "no pain, no gain" type, but they had too long been accustomed to comfort to have affinity for high-performance athletics. These research findings revealed that attributes of a product solution would aid a comfortable transition to exercise from an inactive lifestyle, fitting into current life patterns to the greatest extent possible while motivating the user toward more activity. One scenario that they developed read as follows:

> *Ted Franklin recently lost his father to a heart attack. He is 44 years old, 5 ft, 10 in, weighing 220 lbs. Although his wife and two kids have been harping on him to lose weight, it took the scare of his father's death to make Ted realize that he, too, will have serious health problems if he doesn't start losing his sedentary lifestyle. He was never the kind to use exercise clubs, and there was no way he was about to sweat in front of those buff kids. Yet he needed some type of motivation to get himself moving again, to keep himself going.*

Phase III: Conceptualizing the Product Opportunity

> *Bob would use a "smart insole" that could record his steps and then use a device like a watch or key fob that would more subtly give him feedback on how many steps he has taken all day, not just during formal exercise.*

Next comes the more concrete part of product development, the part that takes the insights gained so far as a basis for generating actual concepts, attributes that can be built into actual products or services. At the beginning of this phase, the team has only a vague idea of what the product will accomplish; it has no idea of specifics. For instance, the team knew that walking 10,000 steps a day was a nonthreatening approach to exercise that could be achieved in smaller increments throughout the day. They wanted to reinforce the benefits of this "bite-sized" exercise, but they recognized that many different products could achieve such goals. By the end of the phase, the team has fleshed out the concept and has even made early prototypes of it. In between, the team considered many different ideas: indicators on the shoe that change color, a wristband or watch pedometer device, a "shoe garage" that downloads information from the shoe, and a modular shoe system in which worn shoe parts could be individually replaced.

Innovation comes from staying true to the value proposition, and product attributes are determined through the research. The approach is iterative in that multiple concepts are considered, refined, and tested, and then the process begins again, with each iteration becoming more focused as more is learned about the product. All aspects of the product—its form, function, and market reach—are considered and integrated into a single concept. The product's emotional potential is realized, and the brand identity is developed. The process is visual in that all ideas are sketched or mapped out to provide a common representation among the product development team. The conceptualization process is energetic and exciting. At the same time, it is frustrating and grueling, because every attribute identified through research must be translated into a feature that performs as an integral part of the product.

The team looked at the dilemma of how to lose weight and become active, a dilemma for Bob and Ted. After discussing the merits and features of more than 50 concepts, the team worked on the idea of a smart insole, one that would track and record exercise throughout the day. The insole would be plush and comfortable, one that would ease the man toward activity. It would have embedded technology to count steps throughout the day, recording and reporting walking totals so that users can track progress toward daily goals. Insoles would fit in regular shoes, accompanying the men in their existing routines, encouraging them to be ever more active in the course of the regular day. The exercise totals could be transmitted to a key fob, an item that men already carry with them. The insole and key fob are discreet objects, not overt advertisements that show the user to be in need of healthful activity. Finally, New Balance already makes insoles, and the technology of feet and exercise is well within the boundaries of the New Balance brand.

Phase IV: Realizing the Product Opportunity

The technology exists to make an appropriate-priced shoe insert with a stylish key fob that Bob could use to read and record his progress. We know how to price it, design it, and manufacture it. We have a plan to package it and present it in stores with a roll-out strategy and a forecast for sales and profit for the next three years. Bob is happy to be getting into shape. New Balance has a new line of products for a new market for overweight men that will extend the brand and keep the idea of performance and fit. This is a market that has tremendous growth (no pun intended).

At the end of this phase, the concept is detailed to the point that the company can decide whether to move the product to production. This is represented in several ways. A complete and accurate visual model is developed through prototypes, computer modeling, and sketching. The technology is shown to be effective through mathematical and computer analysis and through a working, functional prototype. A business plan that includes market introduction and financials argues the business case. Finally, a manufacturing plan dictates how the product will be produced. Even in this phase, the basis for success lies in the eyes of the stakeholders. Very often, this phase can be compromised by a premature commitment to the product, a seductive feeling that the product will be a success, where internal groups rush to judgment without gathering or properly assessing customer feedback.

In this phase, each feature of the concept is detailed individually and as part of the overall product assembly. The cost and manufacture are balanced with the experience of using the product. So the team must work together in an integrated manner to combine the technology and features into a form that not only delivers the technology, but also provides a rich experience of interaction and enjoyment. The product must look as good as it works. It must not only be useful, it must be easy to use. It must naturally fit into its environment of use as well as make that environment function better.

The team designed an insole that functions like any other insole that New Balance makes. But hidden in the heel is a radio frequency-enabled (RF) pressure switch, combined with a microcontroller, that registers each footstep taken by the wearer and enters this data into its memory. This memory is contained within a microcontroller unit, which keeps track of the pressure sensor's input state and stores the daily number of steps for retrieval by a key fob monitoring unit. The number of daily steps taken by the insole is uploaded to the fob, which itself was carefully crafted to be visually appealing as well as discreet. Every insole that the user has in each pair of shoes can be programmed into the same key fob. This device, then, stores the user's total daily footsteps and displays this number to the user, along with other calculated quantities, possibly including mileage, calories burned, or percentage of a goal achieved. This product also includes in its display a graphic representation of the user's progress toward a daily goal. The technology is inexpensive to produce and will not need replacement, because it outlasts the insole in which it resides.

The insole design was prototyped to prove that it worked, analyzed to prove that it would work as promised, and visualized to show what a production version would look like. In sum, it worked, it worked well, it was very well received by the target market in focus groups, and it was ready for patenting. It maximized style and technology and was clearly considered an innovation within its product field. The team did not invent new technology; they invented a new use of the technology and an emotional way to deliver it.

New Balance submitted a provisional patent on this concept, along with five other equally innovative and engaging product concepts that came from teams in the same Integrated Product Development class. New Balance will analyze the business case of each to decide whether to invest in developing the prototypes into manufactured products. The further investment will happen from within, organically growing the company with new market introductions.

As a partnership between the company and university, everyone got a significant return on investment. New Balance received a number of product concepts and details that it could develop into patented products. It also acquired six case studies on the innovation process to help solidify this approach internally throughout the company. The students were given a strong, state-of-the-art process in innovation to take with them into industry, and the faculty had additional examples to demonstrate the process of innovation.

The process laid out in this chapter creates a product that is better positioned for lean manufacture or other programs that assure quality of manufacture. The most critical aspect of quality is the ability to approach launch with complete control and confidence. Any product changes made in the later phases of product development are extremely costly and can affect the ability to deliver quality manufacturing and craftsmanship. By resolving the major issues of a product in the fuzzy front end, the downstream process can more effectively focus on manufacturing and launch.

Today's innovative companies follow a process such as the one described in this chapter to develop new product concepts through the fuzzy front end. These early phases set up the platform for innovation. But these early phases are, for many, the most difficult to navigate. The uncertainty and incomplete information from which decisions must be made are uncomfortable for the traditional breed of engineer and marketer. Yet it is the ability to understand the complete picture of what that information tells you that enables innovation and successful new product development to take place. The tools in this chapter and book are best practices that companies deploy; they are consistent strategies for innovation from within. For that is the approach of the Edith Harmons and Josh Kaplans at New Balance and the Chuck Joneses, Dee Kapurs, and all the others discussed in this book as the new breed of innovator.

10

CREATING A BLANKET OF IP TO PROTECT YOUR BRAND FROM THE ELEMENTS

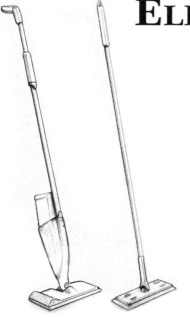

Innovation is as much about design patent protection and trade dress as it is about utility. Realizing early that your best defense is a total intellectual property (IP) offense allows you to keep your brand identity as protected as your technology R&D. Patents are for fixed periods, but trade dress, like a diamond, is forever.

Des Moines, IA. Susan and Steve finally got the dog that Steve had wanted. They had been married six years and had two kids, both finally out of diapers, which was Susan's requirement before they got the pet. For all of Susan's efforts to find a dog that would not shed, when they finally got the mutt from the shelter, it became a crapshoot. Although Susan decided the dog really was cute, it shed like—well, a dog. Susan hated to clean, and Steve was even worse ("Too much to do!"). The twice-weekly cleaning service was fine B.C. (before canine), but A.D. (after dog) the house, especially the floors, seemed to be a constant mess.

In comes Swiffer, that wonderful revolution in floor cleaning from Procter & Gamble (P&G) that has changed the practice and expectations of floor cleaning. Swiffer is not only a trademarked product name, but like Xerox the word has become a verb: "Time to Swiffer the floor." (Not that P&G should like its becoming a verb, but more on that later.) The old drudgery of sweeping the floor is replaced by the easy-to-use dry mop with replaceable cleaning cloths. The cloths use static electricity to grab hold of dirt, dust, and dog hair as the cleaning head sweeps across the floor. The Swiffer mop itself is easy to control and get under those hard-to-reach places with the full pivot action on the head. The cloth makes the process easy with both its minimal resistance as it is pushed and its ability to grab dirt just by moving over the floor. When the cloth is dirty, it is easily pulled off, thrown away, and replaced with a simple motion.

For Susan and every working mom, the Swiffer experience fits right into the trend of cleaning quickly and easily on demand. Rather than making floor sweeping a major ordeal, the Swiffer can freshen up any area of the floor quickly. It is not just for working moms, but dads and kids as well. The Swiffer is so simple that kids can be brought into the cleaning process.

Susan was so impressed with the Swiffer that she bought the companion WetJet, a member of the Swiffer product family that has a container of cleaning fluid that can be squirted on the floor in front of the cleaning cloth for a wet-mop action. The WetJet has done for the mop what Swiffer has done for the broom—replaced it! Instead of grungy mops and dirty buckets of water, the WetJet is clean and self-contained, and only the cloth needs to be thrown away when dirty.

Swiffer: A P&G Innovation Success

For Procter & Gamble, those cloths are important, because that is where P&G makes its money; the mop itself is just a delivery system for the cloths. The idea of constant sale of disposable attachments is a golden one, used long ago by IBM with its computer punch cards and still used today by Gillette with its razor blades. Gillette will happily give you a razor, because you cannot use it without purchasing the blades. Those blades, which can cost a dollar apiece, need to be replaced every week or so. No matter how bad the economy, everyone wants to look good, so they will buy razor blades.

Every industry looks for punch cards and razor blades. Swiffer has found them. Despite all the competitors in the marketplace, and despite the fact that all the cloths are interchangeable, Swiffer is still the category's leader. People Swiffer their floors, they don't Pledge them. Swiffer is a great product. It is also a great brand.

Procter & Gamble is a company that, through its history, has understood strategic growth. By strategic growth, we mean a balance of external growth and internal organic growth. To be strategic, every external purchase and internal development needs to be consistent across the company's core mission. In 1837, William Procter and James Gamble founded the company in Cincinnati, Ohio, by making candles and soap. As the company has grown to be a $51.4 billion company in 2004, almost every product it produces finds its roots in candles or soap. Oddly enough, Swiffer, Pampers, and Pringles all evolved from candles and soap. Candles and soap were natural companion products due to common ingredients—lard and beef tallow from the meat-packing industry.

Oil was used in the manufacture of soap, and in 1901, P&G set up the Buckeye Oil Company for its oil, primarily cottonseed oil. It began selling Crisco in 1911 after acquiring U.S. rights to a hydrogenation patent from Wilhelm Normann. The fibrous material left over after the oil was extracted ended up as the basis for the cellulose sponge. Its absorbent qualities were later extended to Charmin toilet paper. Diapers were an extension of the absorbent and soft qualities of Charmin, and thus came the internal innovation in diapers with Pampers disposable diapers in the 1950s. Toilet paper is a type of thin and absorbent paper for use on the body, so Bounty paper towels were another extension. The absorbent qualities of Bounty combined with some innovative chemistry became the basis for the Swiffer cloths.

At times, Procter & Gamble has purchased outside expertise by acquiring other companies. For instance, P&G bought the William T. Young Company, which made Big Top peanut butter. P&G had already been a supplier of oil stabilizers to peanut butter companies and already had part of the expertise needed for its production, but its acquisition gave P&G additional expertise and machinery to produce its peanut butter brand Jif, which it has sold since. An obvious extension from its use of oil for food is the development and production of potato chips. In 1968, P&G introduced Pringles potato chips, a product that was developed in-house. A less obvious direction was the 1999 acquisition of Iams dog food. Again, P&G already had related expertise, because dog food includes fat. The purchase of Iams was strategic; P&G noticed it could use that domain for additional product introductions that would use expertise it already owned for human products, like tartar-control dog food.

Over its more than 160-year history, P&G has developed innovative brands and purchased other established brands based on analysis that stems from the initial core products of soap and candles. During times of acquisitions, P&G has not been immune to or afraid of growth through purchase of other companies or product lines. While Westinghouse was buying CBS, leaving its core instead of reinventing it, a path to its eventual demise, P&G stayed true to its mission.

P&G also has developed new products from within its extensive and talented R&D group. In recent times, in particular, under the direction of CEO A. G. Laffley, the drive for internal growth has been dominant. Laffley and P&G recognize that innovation is today's differentiator.

This commitment by Laffley to holistic "360-degree innovation" and complete system delivery has led P&G in recent years to develop a strong internal industrial design team, thus adding industrial design to its already strong marketing and engineering groups. The company still uses industrial design, brand identity, and product development firms for the majority of its form and interface work and even some full product development. However, the growth of an internal design team allows the company to develop and keep internal expertise on critical project initiatives with a better connection to the internal understanding of the corporate brand identity. The internal design commitment sends a clear message that the interface and communication of the product as a system are a critical aspect of innovation, a core of the company's future. The balance of internal and external expertise is a current challenge facing many companies and is discussed further in the next chapter.

Why Is Swiffer Out Front?

P&G created an entire system around floor sweeping through the Swiffer brand. But the Swiffer sweeper system is not the only one out there. S.C. Johnson's Pledge Grab-It is a competitive system that was introduced the same month. It seems like there is no difference between them for the average person. Why, then, is Swiffer the brand of choice? Why do consumers so often refer to competing products as Swiffers, but nobody refers to the Swiffer as a Grab-It?

There are many parts to the answer. First, Swiffer was first to market, and P&G made a bigger deal of the product introduction. The market pioneer often gets an advantage in product and brand recognition. Even so, Pledge's dry sweeper was introduced less than a month later, not giving Swiffer much time to establish a stronghold in consumer's minds.

Second is the strong advertising campaign by P&G, which was barely matched by the competition. In part, the first of a new type of product must do the dirty work of educating consumers, so additional advertising is needed. A "me too" product competes for consumers who already know what it does. But again, Pledge came out in the same month. In talking to industry experts, no one really anticipated the level of success from this product, and it may be that the competitors decided to spend their advertising dollars on other products in their strategic portfolios.

The third reason that Swiffer became the market leader and maintains that lead is because of its intellectual property. Intellectual property (IP) is a key strategic differentiator for a company. Many times, it is not the company's products, infrastructure, workforce, or customer base that separate it from the competition, but its IP. Around the globe, countries recognize the power and importance of IP and provide legal means to companies to protect their know-how through the legal system.

IP: Utility Patents

The judicial system believes that, in general, everything that is made or described can be copied by anyone else. The exceptions are those that are protected through IP law.[1,2] There are several aspects to legal IP protection. From a product development viewpoint, these can be divided into technology and style. On the technology side, utility patents protect innovation in functionality and manufacturing. Utility

---

1   Seventh Circuit Court of Appeals. *Thomas & Betts Corp. v. Panduit Corp.* 65 F.3d 654, 1995.

2   *L.A. Gear, Inc. v. Thom McAn Shoe Co.* 988 F.2d 1117, 1993.

patents are the most widely understood and well-used IP tool in new product development. The benefit of a patent for a company or individual is that the government basically gives you a limited monopoly on the use of the technology. The monopoly is narrow in scope, described by the claims in the patent, and limited in time. In the United States, for example, the utility patent is valid for 20 years from the date the patent application is submitted to the patent office.

The Swiffer has two utility patents: one for the overall mop system and one for the cloths. P&G has held additional related patents that go back 25 years, already expired but providing the foundation for the Swiffer product and innovation. The patents for the Swiffer focus on the mop system, including how the mechanism attaches the cloths to the mop head. WetJet has an additional four utility patents focused on the mop structure again, but with a fluid reservoir and fluid dispenser for the cleaning soap. For the WetJet, the patents also specify the cloths, with a cleaning and absorptive layer having certain absorptive properties specified in the patent.

But there is more to the Swiffer than how it functions. Most people think of utility patents when they hear about patents or IP protection. However, the style attribute can provide a powerful layer of protection for a product or service as well. The look, brand, and general association between the product and customer all can be protected. In practice, there are several different methods for protecting the style of a product or service, including design patents, copyright, trademarks, and trade dress.

IP: Design Patents

The design patent is the companion to the utility patent. Design patents protect the form of an "article of manufacture." Design patents protect the effort to create aesthetic innovation. They are simpler to formulate than utility patents and are as vague as a utility patent is precise. The design patent is a sketch or two of a design. If another design looks like the one drawn in the figure, it is in violation of the patent. A design patent generally has a more subjective interpretation, relying on an aesthetic viewpoint. Because design patents are relatively simple to formulate and much less expensive than a utility patent, one technique that companies use is to not only protect the final design form, but to also protect a satellite of concepts used in the development of a product form. Every major form concept considered can be patented. This design patent protection strategy was a technique used by Black & Decker in protecting the SnakeLight hands-free flashlight and proved effective in litigation against several knock-off products.

In contrast to a design patent, a utility patent is precise, and expert wordsmiths craft the claims. For example, if the claim includes a word such as *handle*, as with the Swiffer utility patent, a legal challenge might question what the definition of *handle* really is! Although it is much more expensive than a design patent, companies still create layers of protection through satellite patents, much more strategically and generally building off the main patent.

The Swiffer has two design patents on the dry mop and two more on the WetJet. The design patents for the dry Swiffer show the form of the entire mop system, including the textured handle, long pole, and flat head. The pivot function is not relevant to the design patent, but its integrated look is. The additional patents for the WetJet focus on the look of the grip and the reservoir.

Although in the United States, utility patents last for 20 years from the date of submission to the patent office, design patents last only 14 years from the time the design patent is granted. The courts seem to recognize that styles change quicker than technology. In some industries, such as clothing and fashion, both utility and especially design patents are used sparingly because every six months or less a new style is introduced, making it difficult for competition to remain current even without patent protection.

Once a patent expires, anyone can produce a product that functions or looks exactly like that described in the patent. Savvy companies will submit new patent applications constantly as they take an evolutionary approach to innovation surrounding a product, improving features and updating styles to maintain the competitive edge.

IP: Copyright and Trademark

Companies use copyright and trademark protection for works of authorship such as music, writings, art, and forms (the copyright), and any words, names, and symbols that indicate the source of the product, such as a logo (the trademark). In the United States, copyright protection lasts as long as the author is alive, plus 70 years. For corporate authorship, it lasts 95 years from first publication or 120 years from creation, whichever is shorter. Many core products, such as books and music, can only be copyrighted. The trademark, on the other hand, can be very important for brand protection, and as long as you use it and maintain it, you can renew its protection indefinitely. But it must be maintained. If it becomes a generic word, it is no longer a trademark. *Nylon* and *aspirin*, for instance, were once trademarks but are now part of the normal English lexicon. So P&G does not really want the public to go too far in making a verb out of Swiffer, because then it would not be able to keep its trademark. A way to avoid loss of a trademark is to create two names for a new product—a trademarked name and a generic name, such as Nutrasweet (trademark) and aspartame (generic). The trademarked Swiffer logo, sweeping across the product's package, creates a memorable connection between the product and the person who purchased it. For many product designers, the importance of trademarks is not well recognized. Similarly, for many engineering-focused companies, the importance of brand is also undervalued, as is discussed further later.

IP: Trade Dress

Copyright and trademarks do not address the look of the product itself. A powerful emerging approach to protect the look of a product over the long term is to establish a *trade dress* for the product. Trade dress is probably the least understood but most important form of IP protection from a long-term brand benefit. Trade dress is trademark protection for the look of a product or service that associates the product with the manufacturer. It is less specific than a design patent, but similar, broader, and of longer impact. Like a trademark, as long as you use it, you can maintain it. Trade dress associates secondary meaning to the consumer that associates a nonfunctional feature of a product or service to the product or brand in the public's mind. Color is a typical approach to trade dress. Consider the "purple pill," Nexium, which has a purple capsule and three gold lines, or the brown of UPS ("What can Brown do for you?"). Associating the color with the particular brand differentiates the product from the competitors. Because the color, itself nonfunctional, is associated with the particular product, a secondary meaning is established, and no other drug for acid reflux can be purple (especially with gold stripes), nor can FedEx, DHL, or other package shippers use brown as their identifier.

For Swiffer, the darker green box and light aqua coloring for the handle and base are differentiators that identify the Swiffer brand over Pledge, Clorox, and all the others. Trade dress is an approach to protect aspects of a product's brand identity. It takes some time to establish the secondary meaning for trade dress. The company must work to establish that meaning and prove to the court that it intended to create that connection of the package to the product. Companies can show sales success, the amount spent on advertising, consumer surveys, and even consumer testimony as evidence of secondary meaning of the product feature with the product's identity. Think how much Nexium spends telling us that its pill is purple or UPS to remind us that it is brown.

IP: Trade Secret

One other tool in the legal system can be used to protect IP—the *trade secret*. This is an option for some companies that want the competitive advantage only until their product is released, or for those products that cannot be reverse-engineered (harder and harder to protect with today's technologies). A trade secret is protected, obviously, by keeping it a secret, a more and more difficult task in today's environment, where employees frequently are hired away by competitors. Coca-Cola's recipe and Kodak's emulsifiers are examples of trade secrets; no one outside the company knows those formulas. Technologies in fast-paced markets or fashion trends are often kept secret until release, because by the time competitors catch up, the technology or style will be outdated. The composition of the Swiffer cloths might have been a candidate for trade secret. However, the technologies available today for reverse engineering mean a high likelihood that a competitor would create an equivalent cloth quickly. As it stands, although each cloth is actually different in performance, without a pointed advertising campaign the average consumer will never know the difference between the several cloths available in the market.

IP: Provisional Patents

The cost of submitting a utility patent is high, requiring attorney fees, time from the inventors, and document fees. However, many companies need to discuss their concepts with others to assess their value and the potential payoff. Provisional patents are an inexpensive way to provide a year of protection, after which a full utility patent is submitted; if the full patent is not submitted, all protection is lost. The provisional patent is an excellent way to assess the concept but also is a way to protect its patentability through inadvertent disclosure. Although in the United States an invention that is disclosed is protected for one year before the patent must be submitted, public disclosure sacrifices patenting rights in many countries, including Europe and Japan. The provisional patent, however, is considered protection from disclosure.

Provisional patents are also a powerful tool for start-up and small companies. Not only do they give a company a year to make sure that the investment is worthwhile, they also give those companies that year to bring in the financial resources to pay the patenting costs. A new company often counts on revenues or funding within a year's period, but the early years are also the critical ones to build the IP necessary to compete and differentiate in the world of innovation. Provisional patents are a strategic tool to enable protection of that IP.

Using IP for Brand and Product Life Cycle

The goal of a great brand is to leverage IP for the long term. If secrets can be kept, the IP never expires. But there are other ways to achieve IP benefits after patent expiration. A strategic approach initially protects a product's hard functional and manufacturing qualities with utility patents and its soft aesthetic aspects with design patents over the length of their award period. During that time, the goal is to build consumer recognition of the product and brand and develop an emotional tie to the product. Trademarks and copyrights help build recognition that is then carried over to trade dress. When the patents are no longer valid, the product's brand recognition and association, captured by the trade dress, will be strong enough to carry the majority of the market share as competitors enter the market. The association of the Swiffer colors and package with the Swiffer product connects to the product's brand identity and, because of the product's performance, provides a positive feeling toward the product.

Too many companies don't appreciate the benefits of the full range of IP protection. Many superior technology companies file multiple utility patents with no thought about design protection. Few product developers consider trade dress protection. In the famous legal case *Traffix Devices v. Marketing Displays,*[3] Traffix had made roadside traffic signs under the protection of a utility patent. The patent protected the utility of a spring stand that allowed the signs to be easily placed yet stand up to nature's elements, such as wind and rain. The patent expired, and Traffix then claimed trade dress protection on the look of the spring. It lost the case. Once utility is claimed, nonfunctional elements of style or ornament associated with the manufacturer can no longer be claimed. If Traffix had coated the spring with a color to associate the ornamental aspect of the product with the company, it could have claimed trade dress, and the long association of the color with the quality product might have kept it with a significant market share. However, trying to do so after the patent expires is too late, and the company lost part of its product equity in the market.

Patenting a Product System

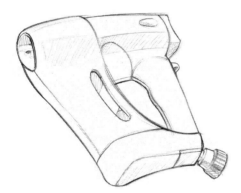

P&G recognizes that innovation today is part of the complete picture of the product. Although focus on technologies yields patentable components, a product is not just the technology but also the delivery and interaction of that technology. For many years, the technology was the focus, the function of a utility patent. In recent years,

3   *Traffix Devices, Inc. v. Marketing Displays, Inc.* 532 U.S. 23, 2001.

P&G has recognized that the style aspect of IP is equally important. It is not just the Swiffer cloths, it is the way people use them—the design of the mop, the means of easily and single-handedly attaching and then disposing of the cloths, the color choice and lifestyle connection of the cloths to the busy person's home life. All of this is supported by IP development and protection.

A recent example of a complete product system is the Mr. Clean AutoDry Car Wash. The innovative cleaning technology, a clear extension of the Mr. Clean brand, enables the car to be cleaned without a bucket and to air dry without leaving a single spot. It's a phenomenal innovation in the drudgery and time to wash and then dry a car. The product uses a patented polymer to clean the car and then a micro shower of filtered water to, in combination with the polymer, enable rapid air drying without spots. The patent-pending filter removes the impurities that cause spots, and the system takes advantage of Pūr filter technology (because P&G owns that brand as well). The product is a complete, patent-pending system that delivers the soap, water, and filtered water in an easy-to-use handheld sprayer, also patented, that attaches to a garden hose. A large button easily switches between the three settings. The sprayer is comfortable to hold, with a purple blue color tone and light lime green accents to lead the user to any aspect that requires interaction. A special filter is designed to easily fit into the unit, and a rubber stop with large pull tab accesses the special soap container. The filter and soap refill each last for about 10 washes, a setup that provides P&G access to a revenue stream analogous to that for disposable razor blades or Swiffer cloths. The instructions complete the system with clear visual communication and engaging, humorous text. For example, in the Frequently Asked Questions section, also available on the Web site, after telling us that the product has a money-back guarantee for an entire year if an unsatisfactory spot is ever left on the car, the question "What will happen to my old bucket and drying towels?" is asked. The answer? "To be honest, the employment outlook for towels is grim…" Most important, the product really works!

As an alternative to making the car wash system, P&G could have sold separate components. It could have sold soap to be added to a bucket and a simple filter attachment to a hose. In that case, the margins for P&G would have been lower. In addition, the lack of a system would have led to a less complete or engaging experience of use, and the likelihood of consumer misuse would potentially have resulted in a poorly washed car and failure of the product.

Patenting Product Manufacture and Delivery

IP and its protection are critical to the success of innovation and organic growth in all types of products and services. This also includes the manufacture and delivery of the product. If you have kids, or grandkids, or just act like a kid sometimes, you probably have visited an amusement park in recent years. As you walked around, you probably noticed and maybe even tried Dippin' Dots, "The Ice Cream of the Future." Dippin' Dots are tiny pellets of ice cream that are served in a dish. They are ultra-cold but melt on your tongue and, amazingly, don't give you that "head freeze" feeling. If you have not tried them, you should; it is a great experience. Because of the individually colored and flavored pellets, the banana split has strawberry and chocolate dots mixed in with the yellow banana ice cream, giving it the flavor and look of a banana split. The cookies 'n cream is especially tasty, with ultra-frozen pieces of chocolate cookies mixed in.

The magic of Dippin' Dots is in its manufacture and delivery, and both are patented. Today more than a dozen patents, including a design patent, protect the IP surrounding that magic. (Also included is a utility and the design patent for a new innovation, "popcorn ice cream"—ice cream that looks like popcorn.) The patents tell us how Dippin' Dots are made. The inventor, Curt Jones, is an expert in cryogenics, the science of producing and using very low temperatures, recently used for the freezing of organs and flesh for medical purposes. Jones took advantage of his knowledge to apply the technique to making ice cream. The cream mixture is dripped in a special way through a very cold (below −100 degrees C) chamber. The cream is flash-frozen into the pellets. The company maintains the form of the pellets by keeping them stored at −40 degrees C. Most freezers are kept at −18 degrees C (0 F), so the storage and delivery system needed to be developed as well. The consistent identity has established brand equity recognized throughout the United States and soon around the world.

Every product requires services to support it, such as the manufacturing and delivery of Dippin' Dots. Every service requires a set of products to support it. Starbucks has several patents covering its roasting process and support products, such as tumbler cups and lids, and quite a few design patents that cover a variety of products, such as chewing gum tins and environmental features such as light fixtures and sconces, all working to define and maintain its brand identity.

IP in Summary

IP-smart companies embrace the full array of tools for IP development and protection. Companies that want to plan for and establish every aspect of protection, including the establishment of trade dress, engage patent attorneys early in the process, not to handcuff the process but to help establish directions where there has been little innovation and IP protection. Regardless of how IP protection is pursued, companies today recognize that international protection of their IP is the best way to encourage and protect innovation from within.

Fundamentally, the reason IP is such an important part of the puzzle is that IP helps define and protect the brand. The technology innovation is protected by the utility patents; the style innovation is protected by the design patents; and the product's identifier, color, package, and general presentation are protected by copyright, trademark, and trade dress, which together define and differentiate a product's brand identity.

11

TO HIRE CONSULTANTS OR BUILD INTERNALLY— THAT IS THE QUESTION

There are many talented product development firms throughout the world, but not all companies know how to integrate outside product development skills with in-house expertise. This chapter discusses how companies can leverage the skills of product developers, both as internal employees and as external consultants. What do they do, how can they do it for you, which firm do you hire, and how do you manage it?

Binghamton, NY. At the monthly meeting with top management, Paul Dinaro was chosen to head the new design initiative the company wanted to develop. The CEO called him in and told him personally, adding that it was possibly the most important thing he could do for the company. The first two things Paul asked himself was whether this was a promotion, and what it meant for his future career. Paul had been in advanced research with a promising career to become VP—if not at the current company, then certainly with a competitor. But his company did not have a history of making design a priority. He was given no instructions, and there were no guidebooks to go to for this one. What to do? Should he find an outside firm to work with? Should he propose a budget to hire a design staff, one focused on product rather than technology, internal to the company? Would he have to be the one to figure out where the budget would come from to pay for all this?

This would be either the most significant growth step in his career or the establishment of his career plateau, and there was nothing and no one he could turn to to figure out which one it was. He decided to give it three months, but he was also going to call his headhunter to put his name back on the active list. The problem is he knew that companies are not plugging management in and out like in the 1990s, so the opportunity for advancement by corporate hopping was no longer the sure way to go.

A big problem from Paul's viewpoint was his company's uncertain commitment to design. The current CEO liked design, but the CEO was relatively new to the company. He had vision, but his vision was not yet part of the company culture; it was still just a vision. He was simply not sure if the company's commitment to design was a long-term one or just in a trial period. The company designed products, sure, but its true technology was focus.

The Power of Design

Problems such as Paul's are pervasive in companies as they seek new paradigms of innovation. Right now, there is increasing interest in product development, and managers are faced with the challenge of changing their company from a project-based one to a product-based one. Businesses have long been familiar with the world of engineering, but business is still learning to understand other members of the product development team, such as the role of product development consultants and industrial designers.

As an example of the evolution of the interaction of business and industrial design, consider how *Business Week's* editorial page editor, Bruce Nussbaum, became interested in innovation. Nussbaum is a frequent flyer, and it was a particular flight that sparked his interest in better understanding innovation. Near him was a mother with a young child, the worst potential challenge to a quiet and uneventful flight. As he anticipated, the child started to cry, and his mother gave him a bottle to quiet him down. Usually, Nussbaum would have settled back in his seat to get back to reading, but he noticed something different. The child was holding the bottle in a unique way. The bottle was split in the middle and formed an integrated handle that the baby could more easily hold than the diameter of a conventional bottle shape. He wondered who was responsible for the innovative shape. The Evenflo bottle Nussbaum had observed led him to become an advocate for good design. As an editor for *Business Week*, he started to write articles about design for the magazine. This eventually led to *Business Week's* sponsorship, along with the Industrial Designer Society of America (IDSA), of the annual Industrial Design Excellence Awards (IDEA).

Nussbaum's groundbreaking articles have been instrumental in expanding the understanding of the role designers play in new product development, and he has probably done more to introduce this type of innovation to the business community than any other contemporary writer. In the summer of 2004, Nussbaum wrote a *Business Week* cover story, "The Power of Design," an article that has struck a major chord in the business world. Along with his role as editorial page editor, he has been the design editor for the past decade. Even though his articles have always helped connect design and business, this article somehow made a deeper penetration than the others. The timing of the article recognized the emerging theme of design and innovation as the new force in American business and major corporations throughout the world.

Using Product Development Consultants

This chapter is devoted to the struggle that companies face when deciding whether to hire external product development consultants, internal staff, or both. Because the best approach is "both," the real issue is to understand what to expect from external consultants and internal employees. Although the internal-versus-external issues apply to consultants other than those who help with product development, the nature of our subject matter leads us to narrow our focus. Though product development requires integrated contribution from engineering, design, and marketing, at times in this discussion we focus even more narrowly to discuss industrial design in particular, because this component is still the least known to traditional business audiences in spite of increased interest in design.

Paul's dilemma, shared earlier in this chapter, is one that managers in many companies face. We have seen companies struggle with the decision of who to hire, how to hire, where to hire. One midsized company spent significant resources looking for a manager of interaction design, a new position because there was only one industrial designer on staff. This company was shifting its resources toward the direct consumer purchase market, and it realized it needed to be more customer-focused. Design was a competency the company had always purchased through consultancies rather than developed internally. This new hire would get the chance to build the in-house team and to work with external consulting groups. The management hired a senior designer who had experience in consumer electronics. But the company did not quite understand how to integrate the new design focus with its existing skills and capabilities; nor did the firm even know what inputs were needed for design or what outputs to expect from it. For instance, the design manager was well-paid, but the company did not make the financial commitment to hire needed support staff. Nor did the design manager know how to work in the existing company culture of engineering and marketing; he was accustomed to working with design peers. As the newly hired design manager began to instill change into the existing culture, the engineering group resented the new approach and environment. The design manager alienated the marketing group by usurping their previously held responsibility of hiring and working with design firms; he requested that all design services, internal and external, be coordinated by him. As a result of the internal conflict, he ended up leaving his position, putting the company in the position it was in just three months earlier.

Another example we have seen is a company that chose to work with a well-recognized design consulting firm on a major product redesign. For some reason, the product (not technology) that the consultants designed just did not work well. The core product was designed with an integrated add-on feature. Most of the consumers would purchase the product with the add-on, but the company also had to compete with a core stand-alone product for trade show comparisons. The consulting firm designed the add-on element but did not create a look that would have made the combined product as elegant as the base, the product itself. This was a classic case of something lost in translation. A thorough brand analysis conducted for the company was not given to the consulting firm, so the new product did not create continuity with the look and feel of an existing product. In addition, the interface, which is so critical to the product's use and acceptance, was also disconcerting in relation to the required performance of the device. Was it the fault of the consultancy or the company? It turned out to be the fault of both. The company did not properly articulate the product requirements. The marketing group that hired and directed the consultancy was hands-off from the technical and interaction requirements, and the engineering group didn't deliver the correct details to the consultants. The consultants took what was given to them with little question or further research of their own to understand the full context of the product's use. No department took responsibility for the whole project—only for "its" part.

These brief situations highlight some of the trade-offs of building in-house design groups and the proper use of external product consultants. Some companies have achieved this balance. Whirlpool creates in-house teams committed to becoming experts who can support the wide range of needs of a particular brand. At the same time, Whirlpool's VP of Global Brands, Chuck Jones, has success-fully partnered with the best design consultancies in the world. This allows him to complement the internal knowledge and understanding of other internal organic capabilities with the awareness and methods of the best outside talent. Jones realizes that complacency is the danger of relying solely on in-house groups and that lack of continuity with the company and market is the inherent challenge with consulting groups. If blended properly, the strength of both can keep a company in the best state of innovation.

Some companies exclusively hire external consulting groups to turn their technology into complete-product solutions. This is especially true of small companies that cannot afford the resources to hire an in-house staff. The first step in properly using consultants is to understand their capabilities and methods. To help with your understanding of product consultants, we describe what is arguably the most recognized product consultancy in the United States and possibly the world: IDEO.

Nussbaum's *Business Week* cover story article also focused on IDEO, because it is clearly one of the most exciting product design firms in the world today. In the broader eyes of business, IDEO's success has repositioned design consulting firms from being extraneous services companies to being core players in the innovation process. According to Nussbaum, IDEO and other similar consultancies combine a new approach to mining customer insights with a more effective integration of translating those insights into product criteria and product form. This process, if coordinated properly, strengthens a product's position in the marketplace, clarifies its brand identity, satisfies the end customer and other stakeholders, and generates greater profit. It is the process of innovation as used by Dee Kapur, Chuck Jones, and Edith Harmon from Chapter 1, "The New Breed of Innovator." If companies such as New Balance, Whirlpool, and Ford are using the process of innovation and are seeking to grow organically, why do they also work with consultants?

Organic growth does not mean that every aspect of expansion needs to happen from within. It does mean that growth needs to be consistent throughout product lines and that new directions need to be understood, embraced, and championed from within. Organic growth is not about who performs the work; it is about whether the growth in the company is consistent with its identity and abilities. Sometimes new abilities need to be grafted on; the scenario at the beginning of this chapter illustrates the possible dilemmas when that happens.

IDEO: The Starbucks of Product Design

IDEO is now one of the biggest design consulting firms in the world, but it competes with companies such as Accenture and McKinsey in influence if not in economic scale. IDEO is a design firm for giants such as Procter & Gamble, Hewlett-Packard, Eli Lilly, and Pepsi and little-known companies such as Zinio, ApproTEC, and Picaboo. An

ABC *Nightline* show titled "The Deep Dive" exposed the company to the world at large, featuring IDEO's redesign of a shopping cart in one week's time. IDEO has also worked on sophisticated medical equipment, designed special effects for movies, and developed toys for children at all cognitive levels and types of activity.

IDEO, now an international consulting company with offices in Munich and London, has its world headquarters in Palo Alto, a city a short distance from San Francisco, where many design consulting firms started in the 1970s and 1980s to support the rapidly exploding digital age in Silicon Valley. IDEO was founded by David Kelley in 1978 with an engineering focus. The company soon found itself in the middle of three-way product trade-off negotiations between itself, its clients, and the industrial design firms that were also hired for projects. The focus of many of these battles was the tradeoff between aesthetics and technology. The clients finally turned to Kelley to ask him to just deal with the whole issue. At the time, he was good friends with Bill Moggridge, head of ID Two, an industrial design consulting firm. Moggridge was a pioneer in the new field of design for digital products. He coined the term *interaction design*, which has since evolved into one of the biggest new areas of design, involving the fields of computer science, human-computer interaction (HCI), and communication design. Kelley and Moggridge were also friends with Mike Nuttall, another industrial designer who had spun off his own firm from ID Two. Kelley's view, and the one he used when first starting his business, was that if he were going to expand his capabilities, he would work with friends and enjoy the process. In 1991, he approached Moggridge and Nuttall with his idea, and together they formed a left brain/right brain combination that would lead to the biggest design consulting firm in North America. The combined effect was far greater than the sum of the parts. This was one of the early examples of merging engineering and industrial design into a comprehensive product development consulting firm. Over the past several years, IDEO has evolved beyond product design into a consultancy that designs services, environments, and digital interactions.

IDEO provides qualitative market research, helps companies talk with their users, and teaches companies how to be more innovative. One of its biggest clients is P&G. Not surprisingly, P&G's CEO A. G. Laffley is one of IDEO's biggest fans.

Raised in a blue-collar town in Ohio, David Kelley studied electrical engineering in college. Like Kapur, Jones, and Harmon from Chapter 1, Kelley has a balanced comfort between art and science. He chose to study at Carnegie Mellon because the school had a top engineering program and a top art program. He was a generalist who never wanted to dig narrowly deep into a field of engineering. Instead, he took many art classes and was exposed to the multidisciplinary atmosphere that has been the hallmark of the university (again, the theme of innovators having that balanced left and right brain). After finishing school, he worked at Boeing and then National Cash Register and then went to Stanford for a unique (at the time) master's degree program that combined engineering with an industrial design-balanced creative approach. The program stressed creative qualitative problem solving and gave Kelley an entirely new dimension to add to his engineering education to date. He then became a doctoral student during the Silicon Valley boom. He found himself consulting with all the high-tech companies and soon decided that product development practice was more his calling than an engineering Ph.D., so he formed IDEO.

Soon after forming his new company, Kelley and his team designed the first mouse for Apple. The core technology had been invented at SRI (Stanford Research Institute), but it was too unwieldy to use, too expensive, and too prone to failure to be sold in high quantities. Kelley's group focused on interaction of use and production and developed a mouse that could be cost-effectively manufactured with subtle ergonomic features, such as covering the ball in rubber. No one had ever held an interface to a computer in their hands before, so it was a new world. Today, IDEO has more than 400 employees and has designed thousands of products.

There are many reasons for IDEO's success. Kelley says that real innovation comes from understanding humans and their needs as individuals and groups. IDEO's approach is to understand how people interact with the world around them and to balance that with technology and business points of view. IDEO hires a wide mix of people with a variety of backgrounds. Social scientists, for example, are key to understanding real users and real needs. At IDEO, the culture of innovation is above all else.

To enable that culture, IDEO hands over responsibility to the work teams. IDEO is divided into small groups, each of which is responsible for its own profit and loss, which directly affects bonuses. In IDEO's view, the more decisions that teams can make themselves, the better. People need to control their own decision space and understand those parts that they cannot control. If a boss dictates the rules, the team cannot understand them or be part of them, preventing buy-in to the philosophy of the rules. When IDEO is called in to a client organization to audit its innovation capabilities, hierarchical structures are often the main deterrent. As Kelley says, "Creative people don't like the boss' boss' boss affecting their lives." Rules lead to less creative cultures. Put differently, giving teams responsibility sets up the proper incentives for them to perform. In IDEO, for example, a team is responsible for its own rules on coffee clubs. If coffee is free, the team's profits are down, but free coffee is a benefit that encourages interaction. On the other hand, if the team charges for coffee, that money can be used to buy equipment, improve the office environment, or be donated to charity. Although this example is seemingly trivial, this and other more far-reaching decisions are made by each group, empowering the team members to create the environment in which they want to work.

IDEO also believes in an innovation process that provides a framework for design without precisely dictating each step. The team does need to work through specific steps to accomplish the process goals laid out. But each step cannot be so precisely specified that there is no, or even little, room for exploration and change. The process IDEO uses must be as dynamic and innovative as the results. This does fly in the face of most companies, which look for and try to lock onto one process that must replicated. IDEO even finds itself adapting the best practices from its client companies and others to improve its own innovation process.

Finally, Kelley says that the biggest deterrent from innovation is fear. If everyone is afraid of being fired, of having your boss or even colleagues chastise you for mistakes, you move to survival mode with layers of protection. When you are in survival mode, where you don't want to make mistakes, you are no longer innovative, because innovation requires risk.

The Consultant Menu

IDEO for product design is like Starbucks for coffee. Other great product development firms exist and can be hired. Many predate IDEO. But IDEO has created a brand and quality level that is recognized throughout the world. It offers a premium product at a premium price. It keeps innovating, offering new skills and services for its clients. Pittsburgh, home to two of the authors, has several Starbucks coffeehouses. But there are also a suite of other excellent choices, local brands that have followed Starbucks' lead but created their own personality and product offerings. Many services of these coffeehouses are good, just as good as Starbucks (if, at times, not better), or offer an interesting variation. But none of them offers the range of goods or consistency in experience that one finds in Starbucks throughout the world. Many of them are less expensive than Starbucks.

The same is true for product design firms. IDEO is the spearhead of a movement that is sweeping the best companies and product consulting and strategy branding companies. Many talented product development firms throughout the world and in every local community offer creative and complete services, even if they don't have the visibility of IDEO. For many companies, local product development firms can provide services that otherwise are not afforded through in-house support. Many of the larger firms can provide insights and results that establish a strong brand presence in any market.

Not all companies can afford to hire IDEO, but all companies can afford many local specialty firms that can similarly provide high-quality services that meet the needs of a growing organization. What is important is to recognize that, whether grown in-house or pur-chased externally through consultants, these capabilities are critical to the success of innovation-driven companies. Recall the problem that the company discussed earlier in this chapter had with its lack of communication with its consultants. Whether innovation is sought in-house or externally, a company must understand the tools of innova-tion to succeed.

So, what are some of the various product-related consultants? What can they do for your firm? An ad agency controls all channels of communication, including print, Web, and television. It also coor-dinates communication design services. You might want to hire a brand development company that specializes in branding. It focuses on a company's identity and branding message and overlaps with advertising companies on the services they provide. Branding firms focus more on identity, whereas advertising firms focus on the distri-bution of your message. There are product development firms that vary from turnkey consultants who can do every phase for you, such as IDEO and Product Insight (discussed next), to specialists who are engineering-focused or industrial design-focused. These services vary significantly. Engineering firms tend to be highly specialized by area, such as heat transfer or structures, diagnostics, and manufacturing. Industrial design firms vary by type of product and scope of service. Some industrial design consulting firms specialize in medical prod-ucts, and others in toys, and some other firms focus on consumer products, computers, and digital equipment. Still other firms just specialize in point-of-purchase or even trade show booth design. The trend for most consulting firms is to try to offer a greater range of design services. Many industrial design and engineering groups are merging and offer full product development services. The biggest product development firms also provide research, packaging, and point-of-purchase design. Many other firms offer communication and graphic design services. These companies can design logos and identities, but at a different scale and cost than branding companies. Some firms just specialize in Web design.

Product Insight: Customer Research and Design

An important element that should underpin any of the tasks mentioned in the previous paragraph is customer/user research. Some hired consultants expect that the firm will provide the research, whereas other consultants conduct the research themselves. The research itself can even be outsourced; there are firms that specialize in the type of research that is critical for product insights, like ethnographic tools developed by anthropologists. Ethnographic methods include observation, in-depth interviews, and other methods of qualitative user research. These techniques are complementary to marketing tools and are especially effective in the early stages of product development and for maintaining a healthy dialogue with customers. Companies vary significantly on how well they integrate these consumer research techniques with the standard quantitative large sample techniques traditionally used by marketing.

Consider Product Insight in Boston. At Insight, Elizabeth Lewis heads one of the largest customer/user/people-centered research groups in the United States. Most projects at Insight start with Lewis and one of her teams. Lewis is an ethnographic researcher. She has her degree in anthropology and started her career under the direction of Liz Sanders, one the pioneers in the field of product ethnography, while working at Fitch in Columbus, Ohio. Fitch did some landmark work with companies such as Xerox and Texas Instruments. Both Lewis and Sanders left Fitch, Sanders starting her own firm, Sonic Rim, and Lewis moving to Boston to work at Product Insight.

Product Insight is one of the few companies that can routinely sell its product research as a core competency. Although Insight is a complete product development firm, companies often just hire it to conduct research to find emerging opportunities. Lewis learned to apply her anthropology education to design better products and services. She went from studying subcultures in a nonapplied context to using her education to determine how to design better products and services. She also learned how to effectively hand off research insights to a product development team. One difficulty many firms have is making that conversion, understanding how to convert the product research findings into features and form. Their process is similar to IDEO, and Insight realized that the research teams should have industrial designers and engineers as well as psychologists, sociologists, and anthropologists. Many industrial designers can conduct product research because they have backgrounds in human factors. But they also have excellent observation skills. Social scientists are trained to observe human nature and infrastructure and convert those findings into observed patterns and tendencies of behavior and preferences. Engineers bring an additional perspective to the research through task analysis, functional reasoning, and statistical analysis. Together, the group understands what the product development team needs to turn this research into product or service features and form. No one ever asks Lewis to look for cheap insights to lower the cost of their products. Instead, the group is always looking for observations that will lead to innovative shifts in the way products function or look in a marketplace.

Lewis and her team at Product Insight were approached by the Aearo Company to look for new insights into how people wear respirator masks. The company was looking for a way to use innovation rather than cost cutting to compete with its main rival, 3M. It seems that 3M not only owns the tape and Post-it markets, it also owns, the low-cost end of the respirator mask business. 3M's ability to control the price of material cost allows it to drive the cost so low that competitors cannot compete at a profit. Aearo was wondering how to stay afloat. It did not just hire Insight to design a new mask; Aearo hired Insight because it also has the talented user research group so important for this task.

Lewis and her team observed mask users and had several insights. They studied people who wear their masks extensively throughout the day. It was not a big deal to find out that people hate to put their masks on in the morning and take them off at night. Most masks have thin headbands that tangle hair and put annoying pressure on the wearer's scalp. The surprise came from watching these workers on breaks. Because of the awkwardness, no one wanted to take the mask off during every break. Instead, they slid the mask down onto their neck, moving the tension onto their throat. People can take 5 to 10 breaks a day. Most breaks are for smoking cigarettes, an irony not missed by the team at Insight. The opportunity was to make the mask easier to deal with on breaks, as well as to put on and take off. The solution was an award-winning mask with an ergonomic insight that allowed Aearo to charge more for its masks and get the sales. Product Insight developed an innovative release latch that allows the wearer to release the front of the mask, thereby relieving the tension. Because the wearer lifts the mask back onto the face by closing the latch, the attachment around the head does not have to be made of thin elastic material that pulls over the hair. A cup at the back of the head keeps the mask in the right orientation for closure and helps maintain a more comfortable position while worn. The mask costs more to make, but the profit margin for Aearo is far greater than anything it could have made while trying to compete with 3M by cost.

In the case of Aearo, Product Insight helped save a company and made the respirator mask industry more competitive by driving up the value of innovation. The most important outcome of this design project for the worker is that more people will wear their masks. Compliance with wearing masks was previously found to be a big problem. If a mask design is better and more comfortable, the compliance of employees, and the possible reduction in insurance rates, will more than pay for the higher cost of the mask. The employees' improved working experience may also mean fewer sick days and reduced turnover, both major problems for industries that require respirator masks. The cost implications of these problems have far greater impact on the bottom line than a slight price increase per mask.

Hiring to Balance Soft and Hard Quality

The type of design developed at Product Insight, IDEO, and other top-notch consulting firms is a new level of practice, a meta level above the subfields of design engineering, industrial and communication design, marketing, and computer science. On the one side, there is product design, communication design, interface design, interior design, and architecture; on the other side are computer science and HCI, systems engineering, electrical engineering, mechanical engineering, chemical engineering, materials engineering, and civil engineering. These two categories have long been viewed as polar opposites, with marketing, sales, finance, and strategy somehow living in the corporate space in between. The companies that are making a difference today are taking the structure of the modern corporation and developing a new model, a model in which these disciplines work together in cohesive, semiautonomous teams. It is a model in which people are central, where project teams practically become entrepreneurial start-ups, a veritable set of small companies within the larger company. This approach allows the product teams to get close to the customer. This must all be coordinated in a way that allows the larger corporation to manage the corporate identity and connect in more significant ways to society at large.

We consider two dimensions, or qualities, of innovation—the hard and the soft. Hard qualities are the more traditional engineering qualities, such as manufacturing, technology, environmental, and ergonomic specifications. Soft qualities are the emotion, aesthetic, brand identity, social, and interaction aspects of a product or service—those that integrate into and define lifestyle.

Companies that integrate both dimensions of innovation have a significant competitive advantage. The challenge is to make room for the company's soft-quality aspects—those that create the look, feel, and emotion of products and services. There are several dimensions of soft-quality management to consider. The first is economic. Soft quality is not a cost; it is its own profit center. This psychological and philosophical shift is important. Whirlpool, Nike, Apple, VW, and BMW understand this, and so does P&G. Starbucks started that way. The automotive industry has been working to balance soft and hard quality ever since Harley Earl's new designs for GM in the late 1920s forced Ford to close down to respond to the infusion of design and market segmentation. Other companies tend to go back and forth at the whim of the current CEO, with design growing and shrinking every few years. HP bought Compaq because it could not grow consumer innovation internally. The main thing is that budgets and companies need to be realigned to understand the investment (not cost) of doing business in an emotionally driven world.

Whether developed internally or hired externally or both, soft quality is not seen as integral to corporate strategic planning, nor is it viewed as an essential component of an entrepreneurial start-up proposal for venture capital. Companies are not measured by the ability to be innovative as a subset of economic success. There is a need to develop new types of measures to effectively determine success of innovation and its direct impact on the bottom line. These measures need to be core to the planning of any company, regardless of scale. Investing in innovation will yield return. It is essential to sustained growth and brand continuity. This is not a cost that companies can debate whether to include, but a new line item that must be allocated to support growth. When computers became a standard in business operations, companies invested inordinate amounts of human and technical resources to improve efficiency. During quality initiatives such as Six Sigma, companies also invested heavily in consulting and the development of internal quality policy procedures and human resources to improve manufacture. The need for these initiatives was clear and the principles fairly easy for executives in companies to learn and adopt. Today, companies must invest in soft-quality initiatives to excite customers and integrate into their lives.

Managing Design

The next issue is who leads soft quality in the company. Companies vary on how they manage soft quality. It may be centralized or decentralized. Companies can have one VP in charge or allow division managers to hire and coordinate design and branding as independent agents. A vice president or director from marketing may be asked to take on the design and branding assignment, or a new person from design, branding, or advertising may be brought in. Design and branding may be split with the former under the auspices of engineering and the latter marketing. Most of the senior management in companies today have been taught and worked under hard-quality (manufacturing-based) and cost philosophies. A major problem facing companies today is that few engineers, particularly senior engineers, and few in marketing and sales have the skills to manage the range of product design services, in the broadest sense, that are needed to develop a comprehensive approach to innovative organic product and service development. Yet industrial designers have not been taught how to effectively navigate or manage within the business context. As well, when industrial design managers are hired, they often seem like an immigrant landing in a foreign country. They speak a different language and find a culture that works based on completely different assumptions.

Looking at the military for an analogy, we know that the best strategy of defense is a combination of land, sea, and air (and cyberspace as well). One of the biggest problems in World War II was getting the different branches of the U.S. armed services to work together, never mind to coordinate with the Allies. You would never take a general and make him an admiral. In sports, how many NFL football coaches could manage basketball in the NBA? Many companies think they can do this without hesitation. The ability to grow managers for the new innovation culture is a tremendous challenge facing companies. It is not just adding services, but managing the existing hard-quality divisions with an understanding of the new soft-quality playing field. The Joint Chiefs of Staff have to be intermilitary in their approach to battle to be effective. In World War II, D Day was the biggest logistics event in history, led by Dwight D. Eisenhower, one of the most enlightened military leaders and arguably the definitive new military leader for the modern era. Every company today faces the same logistical and political challenges facing the military. The ability to combine logistics, politics and, from a global sense, cultural awareness into a coordinated strategy is the key to success in global markets.

Some companies have turned to the use of innovation festivals and mini-conferences. Experts are invited to come in and throw buckets of innovation water at thirsty but overworked employees who are forced to add this new demand to an already overburdened schedule. At the least, it means reeducating a significant number of employees and hiring new types of workers. It is not surprising that directors of product programs often find it easier to put their trust in a creative turnkey consultant group. Even with that alternative, the need to manage and direct external innovation teams and connect them with internal brand issues is another type of challenge. The basic question is how many executives are willing to relearn how to manage in an era driven by innovation?

The world of sports offers insights that are an appropriate reference for integrated management. One reminder is the importance of the team, and the other is the role of the coach. Consider the Chicago Bulls of the 1990s. The Chicago Bulls won championships because Michael Jordan was a team player who excelled as an individual for the betterment of his team. When the Bulls won their first championship, it was because Jordan made the perfect bounce pass, not because he made the winning basket. The pass was made in a split second with just the right touch of reverse spin so that John Paxson got the ball at the perfect height and speed to follow through just the way he liked it. The team's precise execution produced the desired outcome. Jordan's success reached its greatest fulfillment when he realized that no matter how good he was, he could not win a championship without helping to make everyone around him the best they could be. As the result of personal commitment and team integration, Jordan not only led the Bulls to six championships, he also became an international symbol of excellence.

Yet it was not Jordan's talent alone that helped the Bulls succeed. For behind the individual players was coach Phil Jackson, who turned a group of talented, egocentric individuals into a high-performing team. Jackson taught Jordan to partner with Paxson, Scottie Pippen, and Dennis Rodman (the "bad boy" of the NBA at the time), among others. Then, Jackson won three more championships with the LA Lakers and the talented egos of Kobe Bryant and Shaquille O'Neal.

The challenge for managing innovation teams is not finding the talented individual Jordans (although they are always welcome), but integrating the existing talent into a high-performing team; that is the management style of the new breed of innovator. Each individual must be recognized for his or her strengths, and each individual must respect the strength of the others. Forget the Donald Trump factor of who is fired and who fits the mold, and get with the Phil Jackson factor: Figure out how to make the most of the talent you have, and produce something extraordinary!

Epilogue

THE POWERS OF INNOVATION—THE NEW ECONOMY OF OPPORTUNITY

The drive for innovation is being fueled at all levels of the human scale. At one extreme, empowered individuals employ their personal resources. At the other extreme, countries develop national programs to support innovation. Innovation is being applied to single products and to the development of cities. You, the reader, work and live on this scale and can innovate to the profit of your world. How can you enhance your own unique abilities and then connect with a team to produce something better than any one person could?

This book is about deconstructing the process of innovation to reveal the steps necessary to develop successful new products and services. It is about opportunity and the new global economy driven by that opportunity. This book is also about people, about the new breed of person who envisions and develops complete products and services and about the people who purchase and use those products. Innovation is pragmatic to product developers and life-altering to the individuals and societies who use the new products.

As society adopts and adapts to a global infrastructure of business, as individuals demand new useful, useable, and desirable products that flawlessly integrate into their lives, as global resource demands change, and as new technologies enable possibilities, innovation will drive a new economy of opportunity. This epilogue focuses on people and opportunities in this new economy, exploring additional examples of dynamics in social, economic, and technological factors at various levels of the Powers of 10, discussed in Chapter 6, "The Powers of Stakeholders—People Fueling Innovation": new individuals, organizations, market segments, regional impact, global economy, and the new renaissance team of innovators.

The Power of the Individual

Sally just started her new job. Her first assignment is to be part of a team to explore potential new business opportunities for her company. Although the company's products are selling well and are its core profit center, all projections predict that profit will plateau. Growth has already leveled off. Sally's team is asked to find new service opportunities using the company's industry expertise from its products. This way, the company's products will still be a part of the company but will be leveraged in a comprehensive strategy for servicing the customer, not just supplying the customer.

Sally will be working on a team of eight people, all from varied backgrounds. Her education has prepared her to work with diverse groups. She enjoys the exchange in teams and always learns something new from the different perspectives of the team in analyzing user research and, in particular, the insights from interacting with those customers. Sally has figured out that you learn not only by listening to and observing customers but also by involving them in the product development process.

It is clear to Sally that the team manager will be great to work for. When building the team, the manager made it clear that she does not want to micromanage. Her role is to support, energize, and optimize the team's capabilities. The team has no idea where they are going, because the mandate is purposely open; they have been given only a sense of the opportunity. Everyone seems comfortable with that general directive, and they are excited about the opportunity to define their own direction. Sally knows that this will be the focus of the next six months of her life. At the right moment in the project, she will start to think about what comes next, but all she can think of now is the potential of the task at hand.

Sally represents a variety of innovators; she could have a degree in engineering, industrial design, information design, human-computer information, marketing, entrepreneurship, sociology, or any of numerous other fields. Throughout the world, universities are graduating the new breed of innovators. They are coming to business opportunities with a new fusion of skills, shaping how products are developed. In the current marketplace, the value of a corporation is increasingly found in its knowledge workers and less in uniquely owned business processes. These workers not only have a core expertise, they are also comfortable working across companies in integrated product/service teams. This fusion of individual and team is a power that will fuel the next wave of innovation.

The Power to Redirect the Company

Xiangyang Wu was told that he would soon leave the company head-quarters in Shanghai to work for two years in the U.S. plant. His job is to help understand the needs of consumers in the United States. He had just finished working with a consultant from the United States who the company hired to teach them how to develop their own products. To date, the company had been a major supplier, man-ufacturing furniture for other companies in Europe and the United States, but it had not entered the realms of product design or mar-keting.

The company's goal now is to develop its own furniture and cre-ate a unique brand and line of products for the United States. Management has decided to bypass the traditional route of starting in low-cost markets and working its way up the quality ladder; the goal is to produce premium furniture from the beginning. Management does not want to undersell the competition; they want to be ahead of the competition by introducing a new style influenced by Chinese heritage.

The company wants to create its own brand. Market trends appear to be in its favor with the growing interest in Asian-influenced products. The challenge is to find the right balance of current U.S. taste and to blend that with the right features of Chinese furniture. Xiangyang is an expert in the history of Chinese furniture, and his new assignment is to become an expert in the emerging tastes of the high-end U.S. market.

China and its companies have arrived on the international stage. The rise of the Chinese corporation brings with it amazing opportu-nities and serious challenges for other companies around the world. The Chinese-as-cheap-labor model has already changed. The German firm Siemens, whose strength has always been its German engineering, now relies on Chinese engineers for many products. The Chinese company Haier has a plant in the United Sates in Camden,

South Carolina, and has already become a significant market player in several U.S. white goods markets. In 2004, the regional government of Wuxi, China, organized an international conference on design. Its award ceremony had more than 25,000 people in attendance. During the conference, a design executive from Haier gave a presentation about his company's strategy for global expansion, revealing how the company already has established product development centers in several countries to acquire a sense of the emerging needs of those markets. These centers have a blend of designers, engineers, and marketing from Europe, the United States, and Asia. The Chinese government is supporting the move of China-based companies from being component suppliers to original design manufacturers. Just as Japanese and Korean companies have accomplished in the past 30 years, China is ramping up economically using global resources and knowledge to accelerate its economic growth. No company today can avoid responding to this new global force. The only true competitive advantage left for companies in the West and across the globe is innovation.

The Power to Expand the Market

Jim Pirkl has "retired" from his job as a professor at Syracuse University, although retirement is really a synonym for a new career. Jim was an early proponent of universal design and coined the use of the word *transgenerational*, a term for products that span the generations of needs. The theory is simple: As you live through the decades in your life, your needs and abilities change. The world already focuses on the development of products and services for youth markets and for people of average or greater physical and mental capabilities. The average person peaks in physical ability in his mid-20s, plateaus in his 30s, and starts to lose ability after that. The rate at which one loses ability is a factor of genetics, environment, personal habits, and accidents and illness. At some point, usually in his 50s and 60s, each individual becomes less physically and cognitively able and starts to need support systems and devices. Pirkl's goal is to slow down the impact of the process by helping develop solutions to living that allow a person to age gracefully in his or her own home.

Jim now lives in New Mexico and has made retirement his new business. His house is featured by AARP (the American Association of Retired Persons) as a model home for people to age into. After half a century of product and service development being focused on the youth markets of 10-to-30-something, the post-65 retirees have become the new market of economic power and consumer expectation. The youth market is still valuable to capture, both for its spending power and for developing long-term loyalty. Buy a Chevy and move up to Cadillac and stay in the GM family. However, with current life expectancies, with the size of the aging baby boomer segment, and with its volume of disposable income, the post-65 market has become an age range worth marketing to.

The Power to Redefine Our Local Environment

At the next Powers of 10 of product development are issues that affect regions. One aspect of regional issues focuses on limited resources and our ability to seek ways to save resources or develop alternatives. William McDonough and Michael Braungart address energy loss and pollution reduction through economically viable approaches. They are creating manufacturing facilities and buildings that eliminate the need for waste inspection. When water coming out of a plant is cleaner than the water going in, the plant is beyond the standards. The environment improves, and the costs of inspection and rectification decrease. The point McDonough and Braungart are making is not to shoot for a world of compliance but to design around the issue altogether. Rather than decide to meet a government-assigned number on pollutants that equates to "not too much damage," they think out of the box and create positive architectural structures that actually participate in the environment they are built in. By focusing on the larger picture, their approach actually saves the company money in the end. To do this means starting with a new way of planning that takes into account more Powers of 10 in the design process.

Two problems with modern buildings are that they often create interior cubicles that block people from getting sunlight, and they use artificial climate control. McDonough designs buildings that allow everyone to have access to direct sunlight with windows that can open to let in outside air. Natural airflow and sunlight help people stay healthier and make for more positive work environments. In addition, the materials most buildings use leach toxins into the air as they age, a major problem for allergies and respiratory issues in general. McDonough and his partners have generated a list of acceptable building materials and developed new ones of their own. Their roof concepts contribute to the environment by becoming natural extensions of the location they are in. The roofs breathe and return oxygen to the environment, they become a home for wildlife and restore the natural balance of the ecosystem, and they insulate sound and temperature for their interiors. Besides better work conditions, healthier employees mean fewer illnesses and lower insurance costs.

Ford Motor Company hired McDonough to redesign its River Rouge plant in Detroit. Originally built in 1917 by Henry Ford to turn raw iron into Model-A cars, the site became an environmental disaster. Beginning in 1999, McDonough led the $2 billion redesign of the complex, making the land prairie again with plants on living roofs. Not only is the environmental impact reversed, but Ford believes the investment will make economic sense as well.

McDonough's next big regional challenge is no surprise. He is part of a U.S. and Chinese team designing new cities in China. The issues that most people have seen as problems, McDonough and Braungart have turned into opportunity. Their approach can be achieved only through innovation and a passion for finding the best possible answers for complex problems. Just ask Nike, Ford, and Herman Miller.

The Power of Shifts in the Global Economy

Ten years ago, the IDEA awards program coordinated by *Business Week* and IDSA went from being a U.S. product design competition to a global competition. The annual spring issue of *Business Week* that describes these award-winning products is one of the best annual showcases of business innovation. When the program committee considered whether the competition should remain an exclusively U.S. competition, they found they had no choice but to make it international, because there were no longer any exclusively U.S. businesses.

Samsung develops products around the world and has developed products in the United States for a U.S. market. It is no longer clear what makes a U.S. product American and a Korean product Korean. The Honda you might drive is manufactured in Marysville, Ohio. New Balance keeps 20 percent of its manufacturing/assembly in the United States, whereas Nike does not. So is New Balance more of a U.S. company than Nike? Is it better for a global athletic sports shoe company to be seen as centered in any one country? The help line for Dell computers is in India, but the corporate headquarters and assembly plant are in Texas, and some of its parts manufacturing is in Asia. Ford Motor Company now owns Volvo and Jaguar, and Daimler clearly owns Chrysler. The concept of the Big Three in the U.S. economy is no longer a reality. It is no longer clear what nationality many of these companies are, and it may not really matter.

The interconnected world marketplace is fundamentally different from that which the United States inherited as a world power in 1945 after World War II, and the needs of consumers are becoming more defined and segmented. Many companies that thrived in the era of mass manufacture and in large predictable markets are strangely caught between outdated and emerging models of product development. Identifying the needs of emerging trends in global marketing and finding innovative offerings of products and services are fundamentally different from figuring out how to develop an assembly line to make an automobile that is cheap enough to afford, or developing a system for distributing electricity in a city. Few people talk about the system that supports cell phones. In the modern marketplace, everyone talks about the look and feel of the phone, its bonus features, and what the service is like. No one is amazed by cell phones; they just expect them to work and fit into their lifestyle. Countries such as India and China went from limited phone access to high saturation as a result of the minimal infrastructure and low cost to create cellular systems. These countries went from the pre-industrial age to the information age almost overnight.

As another example of the new world order, consider Finland. In recent years, Finland has been considered one of the most efficient countries in the world. Finland has the least corruption of any country in the world, it has an exceptionally high literacy rate, and it has a homogenous culture dedicated to being the best at whatever it does. The government has been investing in a program called "Finnovation" to build economic growth and global expansion. The Fins excel in several areas, such as cellular communication, cruise ships, freight lift equipment, logging products, and crafts and aesthetics in glassware and jewelry. The companies in Finland are joining with a collaborative effort of integrated research with universities of design, business, and technology to turn the country into Finland Inc.—a clear instance of knowledge companies helping to create a knowledge country built around integrated innovation.

The Power of the New Renaissance

Companies that develop new products and services do their best to meet the needs, wants, and desires of society today. These needs change, and products and services that meet wants of the past will not perfectly fulfill future desires. No one can predict how society will evolve, but human beings have a hand in directing that evolution through the design of products and services. The common thread that connects the advancement of products and services, such as the OXO vegetable peeler and Starbucks coffee, to technology changes such as the Apple iPod for music delivery, to the Prius hybrid and future alternative-powered vehicles, is that they must be designed! These designs are all part of the human-driven evolution that exists in connection with or in spite of natural evolution. For better or worse, they drive economies of production and consumption. The cycle will not change, and innovation will continue to evolve, because the social, economic, and technological (SET) factors are constantly changing.

These opportunities are complex and multidimensional. Solutions today must be skillful translations of an increasingly sophisticated global market that is informed and educated by an international infotainment network that relays the latest trends instantly to the far corners of the earth. Solutions today require innovation with respect to all aspects of a product—its connection to human emotion as well as its technical ability. No one can afford to be a disciplinary ostrich achieving isolated excellence, because design requires the integration of a vast and diverse set of skills. Just as important as the skills of creating are the skills of understanding others in the context of ever-changing SET factors. A product is developed by people for people. The human dimension is central to the process and to the outcome.

Leonardo da Vinci was part artist, scientist, and engineer. He painted; developed anthropometric data; designed machines for flight, weaponry, mechanical work, and more; and even conducted ethnographic-based studies for his work. da Vinci was more than an inventor, someone who painted, or someone who made discoveries; he has become the symbol of a broader, more expansive way of thinking and working. The term *Renaissance man* has been used to describe him as a person who was the epitome of a period in time when Europe emerged from the Dark Ages, and his ideas represented a multidisciplinary way of thinking. We are in a new economic age that is in need of a new Renaissance in product development, one that leverages multiple minds working in concert. A "Renaissance" image that is more appropriate to our time than "Renaissance man" is that of a "Renaissance team," a group of people dedicated to making the most of the art and science in all that they create and design. The people highlighted in this book as the new breed of innovator understand the power of teams to achieve extraordinary innovation. They were not born innovative, but they learned how to excel as leaders of innovation.

Everyone who embraces the principles and ideas of pragmatic innovation—an interdisciplinary collaboration, a structured process of exploration, a balance between art and science, a focus on experience and fantasy—can grow into this new breed of innovator. Those who understand and practice these principles are the people who will define the directions of new products, who will lead the design of the new experiences that form the global economy of opportunity, and who will inspire others with their vision and understanding of a process that yields extraordinary innovation. These are the people who will design the extraordinary things to come.

INDEX

"Great schools have... endeavored to do more than keep up to the respectable standard of a recent past; they have labored to supply the needs of an advancing and exacting world..."

— **Joseph Wharton,** *Entrepreneur and Founder of the Wharton School*

The Wharton School is recognized around the world for its innovative leadership and broad academic strengths across every major discipline and at every level of business education. It is one of four undergraduate and 12 graduate and professional schools of the University of Pennsylvania. Founded in 1881 as the nation's first collegiate business school, Wharton is dedicated to creating the highest value and impact on the practice of business and management worldwide through intellectual leadership and innovation in teaching, research, publishing and service.

Wharton's tradition of innovation includes many firsts—the first business textbooks, the first research center, the MBA in health care management—and continues to innovate with new programs, new learning approaches, and new initiatives. Today Wharton is an interconnected community of students, faculty, and alumni who are shaping global business education, practice, and policy.

Wharton is located in the center of the University of Pennsylvania (Penn) in Philadelphia, the fifth-largest city in the United States. Students and faculty enjoy some of the world's most technologically advanced academic facilities. In the midst of Penn's tree-lined, 269-acre urban campus, Wharton students have access to the full resources of an Ivy League university, including libraries, museums, galleries, athletic facilities, and performance halls. In recent years, Wharton has expanded access to its management education with the addition of Wharton West, a San Francisco academic center, and The Alliance with INSEAD in France, creating a global network.

Academic Programs:

Wharton continues to pioneer innovations in education across its leading undergraduate, MBA, executive MBA, doctoral, and executive education programs.

More information about Wharton's academic programs can be found at:
http://www.wharton.upenn.edu/academics

Executive Education:

Wharton Executive Education is committed to offering programs that equip executives with the tools and skills to compete, and meet the challenges inherent in today's corporate environment. With a mix of more than 200 programs, including both open enrollment and custom offerings, a world-class faculty, and educational facilities second to none, Wharton offers leading-edge solutions to close to 10,000 executives annually, worldwide.

For more information and a complete program listing:
execed@wharton.upenn.edu (sub 4033)
215.898.1776 or 800.255.3932 ext. 4033
http://execed.wharton.upenn.edu

Research and Analysis:

Knowledge@Wharton is a unique, free resource that offers the best of business—the latest trends; the latest research on a vast range of business issues; original insights of Wharton faculty; studies, paper and analyses of hundreds of topics and industries. *Knowledge@Wharton* has over 400,000 users from more than 189 countries.

For free subscription:
http://knowledge.wharton.upenn.edu

For licensing and content information, please contact:
Jamie Hammond,
Associate Marketing Director,
hammondj@wharton.upenn.edu • 215.898.2388

Wharton School Publishing:

Wharton School Publishing is an innovative new player in global publishing, dedicated to providing thoughtful business readers access to practical knowledge and actionable ideas that add impact and value to their professional lives. All titles are approved by a Wharton senior faculty review board to ensure they are relevant, timely, important, empirically based and/or conceptually sound, and implementable.

For author inquiries or information about corporate education and affinity programs or, please contact:
Barbara Gydé, Managing Director,
gydeb@wharton.upenn.edu • 215.898.4764

The Wharton School: http://www.wharton.upenn.edu
Executive Education: http://execed.wharton.upenn.edu
Wharton School Publishing: http://whartonsp.com
Knowledge@Wharton: http://knowledge.wharton.upenn.edu

Built for Growth
Expanding Your Business Around the Corner or Across the Globe

BY ARTHUR RUBINFELD AND COLLINS HEMINGWAY

If there's one thing that's consistent in today's business world, it's rapid change. So how do you not only stay steady but actually grow—and quickly enough to stay safely ahead of your competitors? *Built for Growth* delivers solutions to create a brand and presence that generates true customer passion, as you lay a solid foundation for long-term success. Author Arthur Rubinfeld was a major driver in Starbucks' unprecedented retail expansion from 100 stores to more than 4000—and its transformation into one of the world's most recognized brands. Here he presents a proven approach to conceiving, designing, and executing your business plan: creating exciting concepts, growing them to fruition in local markets, expanding rapidly, and keeping your brand fresh and relevant as it matures. His revolutionary approach to business strategy embodies strong personal values, promotes exceptional creativity, leverages scientific methodology in finance and market analysis, and brings it all together with "old-time" customer service. Each lesson is clearly distilled with detailed examples from Collins Hemingway, co-author with Bill Gates of the #1 bestseller *Business at the Speed of Thought*. So whether you're seeking to reignite growth or planning your first store, *Built for Growth* will be utterly indispensable. Foreword by Jeff Brotman, Co-founder and Chairman of Costco, the world's #1 warehouse club.

ISBN 0131465740, © 2005, 368 pp., $25.95

Moral Intelligence
Enhancing Business Performance and Leadership Success

BY DOUG LENNICK AND FRED KIEL

Through a combination of research, and original thought leadership, the authors demonstrate how the best performing companies have leaders who actively apply moral values to achieve enduring personal and organizational success. These individuals exhibit moral intelligence: a strong moral compass and the ability to follow it, even in a world that may reward bad behavior in the short run. Lennick and Kiel reveal how dozens of companies benefit from the moral intelligence of their leaders. The authors help you build the specific moral competencies leaders need: integrity, responsibility, compassion, forgiveness, and more. They offer detailed guidance on being a moral leader in large organizations and entrepreneurial ventures, as well as a step-by-step plan for strengthening moral skills wherever you are.

ISBN 0131490508, © 2005, 304 pp., $25.95